Jesus Talks

A Meditation on the Words of Jesus

CREATING A COMMUNITY OF GOSPEL AUTHORS IN A CULTURE
ATTEMPTING TO CONTROL OUR IMAGINATION

JESUS TALKS
Copyright © 2025 by Micah Thomas

All rights reserved. No part of this publication may be reproduced, stored in a retrieval system, or transmitted in any form or by any means—electronic, mechanical, photocopying, recording, or otherwise—without the prior written permission of the publisher, except for brief quotations used in reviews or scholarly works.

This work is a personal translation and interpretation of the Hebrew Scriptures. The translation is based primarily on the Masoretic Text, with occasional reference to the King James Version (KJV) for comparison and stylistic continuity. The KJV is in the public domain.

Every effort has been made to faithfully represent the original Hebrew meaning while making the text accessible and readable in modern English. This is not affiliated with or endorsed by any official Bible translation committee or publisher.

Scripture references taken from the King James Version are public domain.

For questions or permissions, contact: Jesustalksco@outlook.com

PAPERBACK 9798289435972
EBOOK ISBN 9798289435972

DESIGN BY MICAH THOMAS
AUTHOR PHOTO BY PHILIPEPHOTOGRAPHY

SELF-PUBLICATION IN ASSOCIATION WITH KDP AMAZON

\

FOR MY AMMACHY (GRANDMOTHER), LEELA KURIEN – WHO MADE IT A POINT FOR ME TO MEMORIZE SCRIPTURE AND WRITE GOD'S WORDS ON MY HEART.

TABLE OF CONTENTS

THE PURPOSE
MAPPING TOOL

i. THE GOSPELS
Jesus First Words - Age 12 14
Baptism of Jesus by John 14
Jesus Tempted in the Desert 14
Jesus Begins Preaching in Galilee 14
Jesus Teaches in the Synagogue at Capernaum 14
Jesus Calls the First Disciples 16
The Wedding at Cana 16
The Early Signs & Wonders 16
Jesus & Nicodemus 16
Jesus & The Samaritan Woman 18
Jesus & His Disciples 18
Jesus & the Official's Son 20
Calling Levi & John's Disciples Question Jesus 20
The Sermon on the Mount 20
Jesus, The Centurion & The Teacher of the Law 30
Jesus at the Pool of Bethesda 32
Jesus & the Sabbath 32
The Storm, the Possessed Man, the Bleeding Woman, Jairus' Daughter, Blind Men & the Crowds 34
Jesus Sends Out the 12 34
Jesus' Tribute to John 38
The Unrepenting Cities 38
Jesus Praises the Father 40
Jesus, Lord of the Sabbath 40
Jesus' Mother and Brother 42
Parable of Seeds, Yeast, Treasure, & Fisherman 42
Feeding the 5,000 & Jesus Walking on Water 46
Jesus, the Bread of Life 46
Jesus Teaches at the Festival of Tabernacles 48
Jesus & the Woman Caught in Adultery 50
Jesus, the Light of the World 50
Jesus & The Blind Man 52
Tradition and Commandments 54
Jesus & the Canaanite (Syrophoenician) Woman 54
Jesus & the 4,000 54
Various Miracles 56
The Yeast of the Pharisees 56
Peter's Exaltation & Rebuke 56
Mount of Transfiguration & the Valley 58
The Temple Tax 58
Rank & Warning 60
Jesus, The Gate & The Good Shepherd 60

TABLE OF CONTENTS

Confrontation, Prayer, Forgiveness 64
Jesus Sends Out The 72 64
Parable of the Good Samaritan 66
Divorce & Eunuchs 68
Children, the Young Rich Ruler & the Disciples' Reward 68
Sermon on the Plain 70
Preaching & Healing 74
Parable of the Banquets & Intensity of Discipleship 76
Lost Parables 78
The Unrighteous Manager. The Rich & Lazarus 80
Instruction & Ten Lepers 84
The Second Coming 84
Parables on Prayer 86
The Parable of the Vineyard Workers 88
Zaccheus & the Parable of the Ten Minas 88
Jesus, the Resurrection & The Life 90
Jesus Anointed at Bethany 92
Death & Resurrection Foretold 92
James & John's Mother's Request 92
The Triumphal Entry 92
Jesus Curses the Fig Tree & Cleansing the Temple 94
Parable of the Two Sons, Landowner & The Wedding Feast 94
Taxes to Caesar, Marriage & Resurrection, The Greatest Commandment, and the Son of David 96
The Poor Widow 98
Woes & Curses 98
Signs at the End of the Age 102
Parable of the Ten Virgins, Talents, and the Sheep & Goats 106
Woman Anoints Jesus for Burial 110
Greeks Seek Jesus & Foretells His Death 110
Passover: Preparations 112
Passover: Jesus Washes Disciples' Feet 112
Passover: Jesus Predicts His Betrayal 114
Passover: Love One Another 114
Jesus, The Way, The Truth, The Life 116
Jesus, The Vine 118
Sorrow Turned to Joy 120
Jesus Prays in the Garden of Gethsemane 122
Judas Betrays Jesus 124
Jesus Before Annas 124
Jesus Before the Sanhedrin 126
Jesus Before Pilate 126
Jesus Carrying the Cross Up to Golgotha 126
The Crucifixion & the Death of Jesus 126
The Resurrection & Appearing to His Disciples 128
The Great Commission 128

ii. ACTS
Wait on the Holy Spirit 130
The Spirit to Philip 130
Jesus Calls Saul & Ananias 130
The Spirit Calls Peter to Meet Cornelius 130
The Spirit Sends Out Paul & Barnabas 132
Agabus Prophesies Over Paul 132
Paul's Defense to the Jews 132

iii. REVELATION
The Revelation of Jesus Christ: The Message to the Seven Churches 132
The Spirit to the Martyrs 138
The Last of the Bowls of Wrath 138
The New Heavens & The New Earth 138
Eden Restored 138

THE PURPOSE

Jesus Talks invites you to sit side-by-side with the words of Jesus—not just as a reader, but as a gospel author in the making. In a culture seeking to shape our imagination, this book redefines how we engage with Scripture: not merely studying it, but embodying it.

Through thoughtfully selected New Testament passages and intentionally placed lined spaces, this is not a commentary—it's a canvas. It's a place to memorize, meditate, and respond in writing, forming a dialogue between Christ's voice and yours.

The apostles were effective because they knew Jesus' words intimately. This book helps you do the same—through memorization, reflection, and the transformative act of writing. In becoming gospel authors ourselves, we join a community formed not just by hearing the Word, but by living it, shaping it into our story for this time.

HARMONY MAPPING TOOL

Chapter title	MATTHEW	MARK	LUKE	JOHN	ACTS	REVELATION
Jesus First Words- Age 12			2			
Baptism of Jesus by John	3	1	3			
Jesus Tempted in the Desert	4		3			
Jesus Begins Preaching In Galilee	4	1				
Jesus Teaches in the Synagogue at Capernaum		1		4		
Jesus Calls the First Disciples	4	1	5	1		
The Wedding at Cana				2		
The Early Signs & Wonders	8-9	1	5			
Jesus & Nicodemus				3		
Jesus & the Samaritan Woman				4		
Jesus & His Disciples				4		
Jesus & the Official's Son	9	2	5			
Calling Levi & John's Disciples Question Jesus	9	2	5			
The Sermon on the Mount	5-7		6			
Jesus, The Centurion & The Teacher of the Law	8		7			
Jesus at the Pool of Bethesda				5		
Jesus & the Sabbath	12	2-3	6			
The Storm, The Possessed Man, The Bleeding Woman, Blind Men, & The Crowds	8-9	4	8			
Jesus Sends Out the 12	10	6	9			
Jesus Tribute to John	11		7			
Chapter title	MATTHEW	MARK	LUKE	JOHN	ACTS	REVELATION

	MATTHEW	MARK	LUKE	JOHN	ACTS	REVELATION
The Unrepenting Cities	11		10			
Jesus Praises the Father	11					
Jesus, Lord of the Sabbath	12	3	11			
Jesus' Mother and Brother	11	3				
Parable of Seeds, Yeast, Treasure, & Fisherman	13	8	4			
Feeding the 5,000 & Jesus Walking on Water	14	6	9	6		
Jesus, the Bread of Life				6		
Jesus Teaches at the Festival of Tabernacles				7		
Jesus & the Woman Caught in Adultery				8		
Jesus, the Light of the World				8		
Jesus & the Blind Man	20	10	18	9		
Tradition and Commandments	15	7				
Jesus & the Canaanite (Syrophoenician) Woman	15	7				
Jesus & the 4,000	15	6				
Various Miracles		7-8	7			
The Yeast of the Pharisees	16	8	12			
Peter's Exaltation and Rebuke	16	8	9			
Mount of Transfiguration & the Valley	17	9	9			
The Temple Tax	17					
Rank & Warnings	18	9	9			
Jesus, the Gate & the Good Shepherd	18			10		
Confrontation, Prayer, Forgiveness	18					
Chapter title	MATTHEW	MARK	LUKE	JOHN	ACTS	REVELATION

Jesus Sends Out the 72			10				
Parable of the Good Samaritan			10				
Divorce & Eunuchs	19	10					
Children, the Young Rich Ruler & the Disciples' Reward	19	10	18				
Sermon on the Plain			12				
Preaching & Healing			13				
Parables of the Banquets & Intensity of Discipleship			14				
Lost Parables			15				
The Unrighteous Manager, the Rich Man & Lazarus			16				
Instructions & Ten Lepers			17				
The Second Coming			17				
Parables on Prayer			18				
The Parable of the Vineyard Workers			20				
Zaccheus & the Parable of the Ten Minas			19				
Jesus, The Resurrection & the Life				11			
Jesus Anointed at Bethany				12			
Death & Resurrection Foretold	20	11					
James and John's Mother's Request	20	11					
The Triumphal Entry	21	11	19	12			
Jesus Curses the Fig Tree & Cleansing the Temple	21	11	19	2			
Parable of the Two Sons, Landowner & the Wedding Feast	21-22	12	20				

10

Chapter title	MATTHEW	MARK	LUKE	JOHN	ACTS	REVELATION
Taxes to Caesar, Marriage & Resurrection, the Greatest Commandment, & the Son of David	22	12	20			
The Poor Widow		12	21			
Woes & Curses	23					
Signs at the End of the Age	24	13	21			
Parable of the Ten Virgins, Talents, and the Sheep & Goats	25					
Woman Anoints Jesus For Burial	26	14				
Greeks Seek Jesus & Jesus Foretells His Death				12		
Passover: Preparations	26	14	22			
Passover: Jesus Washes His Disciples' Feet				13		
Passover: Jesus Predicts His Betrayal	26	14	22	13		
Passover: Love One Another	26	14	22	13		
Jesus, The Way, The Truth. The Life				14		
Jesus, The Vine				15		
Sorrow Turned to Joy				16		
Jesus Prays in the Garden of Gethsemane	26	14	22	17		
Judas Betrays Jesus	26	14	22	18		
Jesus Before Annas				18		
Jesus Before the Sanhedrin	26	14	22			
Jesus Before Pilate	27	15	23	18-19		
Jesus Carrying the Cross Up to Golgotha			23			
The Crucifixion & Death of Jesus	27	15	23	19		

Chapter title	MATTHEW	MARK	LUKE	JOHN	ACTS	REVELATION
The Resurrection of Jesus & Appearing to His Disciples	28		24	20-21		
The Great Commission	28	16				
Wait on the Holy Spirit					1	
The Spirit to Philip					8	
Jesus Calls Saul & Ananias					9	
The Spirit Calls Peter to Meet Cornelius					10	
The Spirit Sends Out Paul & Barnabas					13	
Agabus Prophesies Over Paul					21	
Paul's Defense to the Jews					22-23	
The Revelation of Jesus Christ: The Message to the Seven Churches						1-3
The Spirit to the Martyrs						14
The Last of the Bowls of Wrath						16
The New Heavens & The New Earth						21
Eden Restored						22

JESUS' FIRST WORDS - AGE 12
Luke 2
"Why is it that you were searching for Me? Didn't you know I was in My Father's house?"

BAPTISM OF JESUS BY JOHN
Matthew 3, Mark 1, Luke 3
Let it be so now; it is proper for us to do this to fulfill all righteousness.
"THIS IS MY SON, WHOM I LOVE; WITH HIM I AM WELL PLEASED."

JESUS TEMPTED IN THE DESERT
Matthew 4 - Luke 3
It is written: 'Man does not live on bread alone, but on every word that comes from the mouth of God.'
On the other hand, it is also written: 'Do not put the Lord your God to the test.'
Away from me, Satan! For it is written: 'Worship the Lord Your God, and serve Him only.'

JESUS BEGINS PREACHING IN GALILEE
Matthew 4 - Mark 1
Repent for the kingdom of heaven is near. Repent and believe the good news.
[to a demon] be quiet! Come out of him!

JESUS TEACHES IN THE SYNAGOGUE AT CAPERNAUM
Mark 1 - Luke 4
The Spirit of the Lord is upon me,
Because he has anointed me to preach good news to the poor, He has sent me to proclaim freedom for the prisoners and recovery of sight for the blind, to release the oppressed, to proclaim the year of the Lord's favor. Today this Scripture is fulfilled in your hearing.Surely you will quote this proverb to me: 'Physician, heal yourself! Do here in your hometown what we have heard you did in Capernaum.' I tell you the truth, no prophet is accepted in his hometown. I assure you that there were many widows in Israel in Elijah's time, when the sky was shut for three and a half years and there was a severe famine throughout the land. Yet Elijah was not sent to any of them, but to a widow in Zarephath in the region of Sidon. And there were many prophets in Israel with leprosy in the time of Elisha the prophet, yet not one of them was cleaned – Only Naaman the Syrian.

JESUS CALLS THE FIRST DISCIPLES
Matthew 4 - Mark 1 - Luke 5 - John 1

Put out into deep water, and let down the nets for a catch. Don't be afraid. Come, follow me and I will make you fishers of men. What are you seeking? Come and you will see. You are Simon, son of John. You will be called Cephas.

Let us go somewhere else– I must preach the good news of the Kingdom of God to the other towns and villages also, because that is why I was sent and why I have come.

[to Philip] Follow me.

[to Nathanael] Here is truly an Israelite, in whom there is no deceit! Before Philip called you, when you were under the fig tree, I saw you. Because I said to you that I saw you under the fig tree, do you believe? You will see greater things than these. Truly, truly, I say to you, you will see heaven opened and the angels of God ascending and descending on the Son of Man.

THE WEDDING AT CANA
John 2

What business do you have with Me, woman? My hour has not yet come.
Fill the waterpots with water. Draw some out now and take it to the headwaiter.

THE EARLY SIGNS & WONDERS
Matthew 8-9 - Mark 1 - Luke 5

I am willing, be clean! See that you don't tell anyone. But go, show yourself to the priest and offer them the gift Moses commanded, as a testimony to them.

Take heart Son, your sins are forgiven. Why are you thinking these things? Which is easier: to say to the paralytic, 'Your sins are forgiven' or to say 'Get up, take up your mat, and walk'? But that you may know that the Son of Man has authority on Earth to forgive sins. I tell you, get up, take your mat and go home.

JESUS & NICODEMUS
John 3

I tell you the truth, no one can see the kingdom of God unless he is born again. I tell you the truth, no one can enter the kingdom of God unless he is born out of water and the Spirit. Flesh gives birth to flesh, but the Spirit gives birth to Spirit. You should not be surprised at My saying, 'You must be born again.' The wind blows wherever it pleases. You hear its sounds, but you cannot tell where it comes from or where it is going. So it is with everyone born of the Spirit. You are Israel's teacher, and do not understand these things? I tell you the truth, we speak of what we know, and we testify to what we have seen, but still you people do not accept

our testimony. I have spoken to you of earthly things and you do not believe; how then will you believe if I speak of heavenly things? No one has ever gone to heaven except the one who came from heaven– the Son of Man. Just as Moses lifted up the snake in the desert, so the Son of Man must be lifted up, that everyone who believes in Him may have eternal life. For God so loved the world that He gave His one and only Son, that whoever believes in Him shall not perish, but have eternal life. For God did not send His Son into the world to condemn the world, but to save the world through Him. Whoever believes in Him is not condemned, but whoever does not believe stands condemned already because they have not believed in the name of God's one and only Son. This is the verdict: Light has come into the world, but men loved darkness instead of the light because their deeds were evil. Everyone who does evil hates the light, and will not come into the light for fear that his deeds will be exposed. But whoever lives by the truth comes into the light, so that it may be seen plainly that what he has done has been done through God.

JESUS & THE SAMARITAN WOMAN
John 4
Will you give me a drink?
If you knew the gift of God and who it is that asks you for a drink, you would have asked Him and he would have given you living water. Everyone who drinks this water will be thirsty again, but whoever drinks the water I give him will never thirst. Indeed, the water I give him will become in him a spring of water welling up to eternal life. Go and call your husband and come back.
You are right when you say you have no husband. The fact is, you have had five husbands, and the man you now have is not your husband. What you have said is quite true. Believe me, woman, a time is coming when you will worship the father neither on this mountain nor in Jerusalem. You Samaritans worship what you do not know; We worship what we do know, for salvation is from the Jews. Yet a time is coming and has now come when the true worshippers will worship the Father in spirit and truth, for they are the kind of worshippers the Father seeks. God is spirit, and His worshippers must worship in Spirit and in Truth.
I who speak to you am He.

JESUS & HIS DISCIPLES
John 4
I have food to eat that you know nothing about. My food is to do the will of Him who sent me and to finish His work. Do you not say, 'Four months more and then the harvest'? I tell you, open your eyes and look at the fields! They are ripe for

Harvest. Even now the reaper draws his wages, even now he harvests the crop for eternal life, so that the sower and the reaper may be glad together. Thus the saying, 'One sows and another reaps' is true. I sent you to reap what you have not worked for. Others have done the hard work and you have reaped the benefits of their labor.

JESUS & THE OFFICIAL'S SON
John 4
Unless you people see miraculous signs and wonders, you will never believe. You may go, your son will live.

CALLING LEVI & JOHN'S DISCIPLES QUESTION JESUS
Matthew 9 - Mark 2 - Luke 5
Follow Me. But go and learn what this means: 'I desire mercy, not sacrifice.' It is not the healthy who need a doctor, but the sick. For I have not come to call the righteous, but sinners to repentance. How can the guests of the bridegroom mourn while he is with them? The time will come when the bridegroom will be taken from them; then they will fast. No one sews a patch of unshrunk cloth on an old garment, for the patch will pull away from the garment, making the tear worse and the new will not match the old. No one after drinking old wine wants the new wine for he says, 'the old is better.' Neither do men pour new wine into old wineskins. If they do, the skins will burst, the wine will run out and the wineskins will be ruined. No, they pour new wine into new wineskins, and both are preserved.

THE SERMON ON THE MOUNT
MATTHEW 5-7 - LUKE 6
Blessed are the poor in spirit, for theirs is the kingdom of heaven.
Blessed are you who are poor, for yours is the kingdom of God.
Blessed are those who mourn, for they will be comforted.
Blessed are you who weep now, for you will laugh.
Blessed are the meek, for they will inherit the earth.
Blessed are those who hunger and thirst for righteousness, for they will be filled.
Blessed are you who hunger now, for you will be satisfied.
Blessed are the merciful, for they will be shown mercy.
Blessed are the pure in heart, for they will see God.
Blessed are the peacemakers, for they will be called Sons of God.
Blessed are those who are persecuted because of righteousness, for theirs is the kingdom of heaven.

Blessed are you when men hate you, insult you, persecute you, exclude you, reject your name as evil because of the Son of Man, and falsely say all kinds of evil against you because of me.

Rejoice and be glad on that day and leap for joy, because great is your reward in heaven. For in the same way is how their fathers persecuted the prophets who were before you.

But cursed are you who are rich, for you have already received your comfort.

Cursed are you who are well fed now, for you will go hungry.

Cursed are you who will laugh now, for you will mourn and weep.

Cursed are you when all men speak well of you, for that is how their fathers treated the false prophets.

You are the salt of the earth, but if salt loses its saltiness, how can it be made salty again? It is no longer good for anything, except to be thrown out and trampled by men.

You are the light of the world. A city on a hill cannot be hidden. Neither do people light a lamp and put it under a bowl. Instead they put it on its stand, and it gives light to everyone in the house. In the same way, let your light shine before men, that they may see your good deeds and praise your Father in Heaven.

Do not think that I have come to abolish the Law or the Prophets; I have not come to abolish them but to fulfill them. I tell you the truth, until heaven and earth disappear, not the smallest letter, not the least stroke of a pen, will by any means disappear from the Law until everything is accomplished. Anyone who breaks the least of these commandments and teaches others to do the same will be called the least in the kingdom of heaven. But whoever practices and teaches these commands will be called great in the kingdom of heaven. For I tell you that unless your righteousness surpasses that of the Pharisees and the teachers of the Law, you will certainly not enter the kingdom of heaven.

You have heard it was said to the people long ago, 'Do not murder, and anyone who murders will be subject to judgement. But I tell you that anyone who is angry with his brother will be subject to judgement. Again, anyone who says to his brother, 'you good for nothing,' is answerable to the Sanhedrin. But anyone who says, 'you fool!' will be in danger of the gehenna of fire. Therefore, if you are offering your gift at the altar and remember that your brother has something against you, leave your gift there in front of the altar. First go and be reconciled to your brother, then come and offer your gift. Settle your matters quickly with your adversary who is taking you to court. Do it while you are still with him on the way, or he may hand you over to the judge, and the judge may hand you over to the officer, and you may be thrown into prison. I tell you the truth, you will not get

out until you have paid the last quadran.

You have heard it was said, 'Do not commit adultery.' but i tell you that anyone who looks at a woman lustfully has already committed adultery with her in his heart. If your right eye causes you to sin, gouge it out and throw it away.

It is better for you to lose one part of your body than for your whole body to be thrown into gehenna. And if your right hand causes you to sin, cut it off and throw it away. It is better for you to lose one part of your body than for your whole body to go into gehenna.

It has been said, 'anyone who divorces his wife must give her a certificate of divorce.' but I tell you that anyone who divorces his wife, except for marital unfaithfulness, causes her to become an adulteress and anyone who marries the divorced woman commits adultery.

Again, you have heard that it was said to the people long ago, 'Do not break your oath, but keep your oaths you have made to the Lord.' but I tell you, do not swear at all: either by heaven, for it is God's throne; or by earth, for it is his footstool; or by Jerusalem, for it is the city of the great king. And do not swear by your hand, for you cannot make even one hair white or black. Simply let your 'yes' be 'yes,' and your 'no,' 'no.' Anything beyond this comes from the evil one.

You have heard that it was said, 'Eye for eye, and tooth for tooth.' but I tell you, do not resist an evil person. If someone strikes you on the right cheek, turn to him the other cheek also. And if someone wants to sue you and take your tunic, let him have your cloak as well. If someone forces you to go one mile, go with him two miles. Give to the one who asks you, and do not turn away from the one who wants to borrow from you.

You have heard that it was said, 'Love your neighbor and hate your enemy.' but I tell you: Love your enemies, do good to those who hate you, bless those who curse you, pray for those who persecute you, that you may be sons of your Father in heaven, He causes his sun to rise on the evil and the good, And sends rain on the just, and the unjust. If you love those who love you, what reward will you get? Are not even the tax collectors doing that? Even sinners love those who love them. And if you do good to those who are good to you, what credit is that to you? Even sinners do that. And if you greet only your brothers, what are you doing more than others? Do not even the pagans do that? And if you lend to those from whom you expect repayment, what credit is that to you? Even sinners lend to sinners, expecting to be repaid in full. But love your enemies, do good to them, and lend to them without expecting to get anything back. Then your reward in heaven will be great, and you will be sons of the Most High, because he is kind to the ungrateful and wicked. Be merciful just as your Father is merciful. Be perfect, therefore, as your heavenly Father is perfect.

Be careful not to do your acts of righteousness before men, to be seen by them. If you do, you will have no reward from your Father in heaven. So when you give to the needy, do not announce it with trumpets, as the hypocrites do in the synagogue and on the streets, to be honored by men. I tell you the truth, they have received their reward in full. But when you give to the needy, do not let your left hand know what your right hand is doing. So that your giving may be in secret. Then your Father, who sees what is done in secret will reward you.

And when you pray, do not live like the hypocrites, for they love to pray standing in the synagogues and on the street corners to be seen by men. I tell you the truth, they have received their reward in full. But when you pray, go to your room, close the door, and pray to your Father, who is unseen. Then your Father, who sees what is done in secret, will reward you. And when you pray, do not keep babbling like pagans, for they think they will be heard because of their many words. Do not be like them, for your Father knows what you need before you ask Him. This then is how you should pray:

Our father in Heaven,

May your name be made Holy,

May your kingdom come,

May your will be done on Earth as it is in Heaven.

Give us today, our daily bread.

Forgive us our debts, as we also have forgiven our debtors.

And lead us not into temptation, but deliver us from the evil one.'

For if you forgive men when they sin against you, your heavenly Father will also forgive you. But if you do not forgive men their sins, your Father will not forgive your sins.

When you fast, do not look somber as the hypocrites do, for they disfigure their faces to show men they are fasting. I tell you the truth, they have received their reward in full. But when you fast, put oil on your head and wash your face, so that it will not be obvious to men that you are fasting, but only to your Father, who is unseen. And your Father, who sees what is done in secret, will reward you.

Do not store up for yourselves treasure on earth, where moth and rust destroy, and where thieves break in and steal. But store up for yourselves treasures in heaven where moth and rust do not destroy, and where thieves do not break in and steal. For where your treasure is, there your heart is also.

The eye is the lamp of the body. If your eyes are good, your whole body will be full of light. But if your eyes are bad, your whole body will be full of darkness and how great is that darkness! No one can serve two masters. Either he will hate the one and love the other, or he will be devoted to the one and despise the other. You cannot serve both God and Mammon [money].

Therefore I tell you, do not worry about your life, what you will eat or drink, or about your body, what you will wear. Is not life more important than food, and the body more important than clothes?

Look at the birds of the air; they do not sow or reap or store away in barns, and yet your heavenly Father feeds them. Are you not much more valuable than they? Who of you by worrying can add a single hour to his life? And why do you worry about clothes? See how the lilies of the field grow. They do not labor or spin. Yet I tell you that not even Solomon in all his splendor was dressed like one of these. If that is how God clothes the grass of the field, which is here today and tomorrow thrown into the fire, will he not much more clothe you, O you of little faith. So do not worry, saying, 'What shall we eat?' or 'what shall we drink?' or what shall we wear?' For the pagans run after all these things, and your heavenly Father knows that you need them. But seek first his kingdom and his righteousness, and all these things will be given to you as well. Therefore do not worry about tomorrow , for tomorrow will worry about itself. Each day has enough trouble of its own.

Do not judge, or you too will be judged. Do not judge, and you will not be judged. Do not condemn, and you will not be condemned. Forgive, and you will be forgiven. Give, and it will be given to you. A good measure, pressed down, shaken together and running over, will be poured on your lap. For in the same way you judge others, you will be judged, and with the measure you use, it will be measured to you. Why do you look at the speck of sawdust in your brother's eye and pay no attention to the plank in your own eye? How can you say to your brother, 'Let me take the speck out of your eye,' when all the time there is a plank in your own eye? You hypocrite, first take the plank out of your own eye, and then you will see clearly to remove the speck from your brother's eye.

Can a blind man lead a blind man? Will they not both fall into a pit? A student is not above his teacher, but everyone who is fully trained will be like his teacher. Ask and it will be given to you; seek and you will find; knock and the door will be opened to you. For everyone who asks receives; he who seeks finds; and he who knocks, the door will be opened. Which of you, if his son asks for bread, will give him a stone? Or if he asks for a fish, will give him a snake? If you, then, though you are evil, know how to give good gifts to your children, how much more will your Father in heaven give good gifts to those who ask Him! So in everything, do to others what you would have them do to you, for this sums up the Law and the Prophets. Enter through the narrow gate. For wide is the gate and broad is the road that leads to destruction, and many enter through it. But small is the gate and narrow the road that leads to life, and only a few find it.

Watch out for false prophets. They come to you in sheep's clothing, but inwardly they are ferocious wolves. By their fruit you will recognize them. Do people pick grapes from thorn bushes, or figs from thistles? Likewise every good tree bears good fruit, but a bad tree bears bad fruit. A good tree cannot bear bad fruit, but a bad tree cannot bear good fruit. Every tree that does not bear good fruit is cut down and thrown into the fire. The good man brings good things out of the good stored up in his heart, and the evil man brings evil things out of the evil stored up in his heart. For out of the overflow of his heart, his mouth speaks. Thus, by their fruit you will recognize them.

Not everyone who says to me, 'Lord, Lord,' will enter the kingdom of heaven, but only he who does the will of my Father who is in heaven. Many will say to me on that day, 'Lord, Lord, did we not prophesy in your name and in your name drive out demons and perform many miracles.' Then I will tell them plainly, 'I never knew you. Away from me, you evildoers!'

Why do you call me, 'Lord, Lord' and do not do what I say? Therefore I will show you that everyone who hears these words of mine and puts them into practice is like a wise man who built his house, who dug deep and laid the foundation on rock. The rain came, the streams rose, and the winds blew and beat against that house; yet it did not fall because it had its foundation on the rock. But everyone who hears these whos of mine and does not put them into practice is like a foolish man who built his house on the sand. The rain came, the streams rose, and the winds blew and beat against that house, and it collapsed, and fell with a great crash, and its destruction was complete.

JESUS, THE CENTURION & THE TEACHER OF THE LAW
Matthew 8 - Luke 7
I will go and heal him.
I tell you the truth, I have not found anyone in Israel with such great faith. I say to you that many will come from the east and the west, and will take their places at the feast with Abraham, Isaac, and Jacob in the kingdom of heaven. But the sons of the kingdom will be thrown out into the outer darkness, in that place there will be weeping and gnashing of teeth. Go! It shall be done for you as you have believed.
Foxes have holes and birds of the air have nests, but the Son of Man has no place to lay his head. Follow me, and let the dead bury their own dead.

JESUS AT THE POOL OF BETHESDA
John 5

Do you want to get well? Get up! Pick your mat and wall. See, you are well again. Stop sinning or something worse may happen to you.

My Father is always at his work to this very day, and I, too, am working. I tell you the truth, the Son can do nothing by Himself; he can only do what He sees his Father doing, because whatever the Father does, the Son does also. For the Father loves the Son and shows Him all He does. Yes, to your amazement He will show Him even greater things than these. For just as the Father raises the dead and gives them life, even so the Son gives life to whom He is pleased to give it. Moreover, the Father judges no one, but has entrusted all judgement to the Son, so that all may honor the Son just as they honor the Father. He who does not honor the Son does not honor the Father, who sent Him. I tell you the truth, whoever hears my word and believes in Him who sent me has eternal life and will not be condemned; he has crossed over from death to life. I tell you the truth, a time is coming and has now come when the dead will hear the voice of the Son of God and those who hear will live. For as the Father has life in Himself, so He has granted Him authority to judge because He is the Son of Man. Do not be amazed at this, for a time is coming when all who are in their graves will hear His voice, and come– those who have done good will rise to live, and those who have done evil will rise to be condemned. By myself I can do nothing, I judge only as I hear, and my judgement is just. For I seek not to please myself but Him who sent me.

JESUS & THE SABBATH
Matthew 12 - Mark 2-3 - Luke 6

Haven't you read what David did when he and his companions were hungry? He entered the house of God, and he and his companions ate the consecrated bread– which was not lawful for them to do, but only for the priest. Or haven't you read in the Law that on the Sabbath the priests in the temple desecrate the day and yet are innocent? I tell you that one greater than the temple is here. If you had known what these words mean, 'I desire mercy, not sacrifice,' you would not have condemned the innocent. For the Son of Man is the Lord of the Sabbath.
The Sabbath was made for man, not man for the Sabbath.
If any of you has a sheep and it falls into a pit on the Sabbath, will you not take hold of it and lift it out? How much more valuable is a man than a sheep! Therefore it is lawful to do good on the Sabbath.
[to the man with the shriveled hand] Stand up in front of everyone. Which is lawful on the Sabbath: to do good or to do evil, to save life or to kill and destroy? Stretch out your hand!

THE STORM, THE POSSESSED MAN, THE BLEEDING WOMAN, JAIRUS' DAUGHTER, BLIND MEN, & THE CROWDS
Matthew 8-9 - Mark 4 - Luke 8

Let's go over to the other side of the lake.
[to the storm] Quiet! Be still!
You of little faith, why are you so afraid? Do you still have no faith?

[to the possessed man] Come out of this man! Go, you evil spirit!
What is your name?
Go home to your family and tell them how much the Lord has done for you, and how he has had mercy on you.

Who touched me? Someone touched me; I know that power has gone out from me
[to the bleeding woman] Take heart, daughter, your faith has healed you. Go in peace and be freed from your suffering.

[to the synagogue official] Do not be afraid, only believe.
[to the mourners] Stop wailing! Go away! The girl is not dead, but asleep.
[to the little girl] My child, get up! (Talitha koum!)

[to the blind men] Do you believe that I am able to do this? According to your faith it will be done to you. See that no one knows about this.

[to the crowds] The harvest is plentiful, but the workers are few. Therefore, plead with the Lord of the harvest to send out workers into His harvest field.

JESUS SENDS OUT THE 12
Matthew 10 - Mark 6 - Luke 9

Do not go among the gentiles or enter any towns of the Samaritans. Go rather to the lost sheep of Israel. As you go, preach the message: 'The Kingdom of heaven is near.' Heal the sick, raise the dead, cleanse those who have leprosy, drive out demons. Freely you have received, freely give. Do not take along any gold or silver or copper in your belts; take no bag for the journey, or extra tunic, or sandals or a staff; for the worker is worth his keep. Whatever town or village you enter, search for some worthy person there and stay at his house until you leave. As you enter the home, give it your greeting. If the home is deserving, let your peace rest on it; if it is not let your peace return to you. If anyone will not welcome or listen to your words, shake the dust off your feet when you leave that home or town.

I tell you the truth, it will be more bearable for Sodom and Gomorrah on the day of judgement than for that town. I am sending you out like sheep among wolves. Therefore be as shrewd as snakes and as innocent as doves. Be on your guard against men; they will hand you over to the local councils and flog you in their synagogues. On my account you will be brought before governors and kings as witnesses to them and to the gentiles. But when they arrest you, do not worry about what to say or how to say it. At that time you will be given what to say, for it will not be you speaking, but the Spirit of the Father speaking through you. Brother will betray brother to death, and a father his child; children will rebel against their parents and have them put to death. All men will hate you because of me, but he who stands firm to the end will be saved. When you are persecuted in one place, flee to another. I tell you the truth, you will not finish going through cities before the Son of Man comes. A student is not above his teacher, nor a servant above his master. It is enough for the student to be like his teacher, and a servant like his master. If the head of he house has been called Beelzebub, how much more the members of his household! So do not be afraid of them. There is nothing concealed that will not be disclosed, or hidden that will not be made known. What I tell you in the dark, speak in the daylight; what is whispered in your ear, proclaim from the roofs. Do not be afraid of those who kill the body but cannot kill the soul. Rather, be afraid of the One who can destroy both soul and body in gehenna. Are not two sparrows sold for a penny? Yet not one of them will fall to the ground apart from the will of your Father. And even the very hairs on your head are all numbered. So don't be afraid; you are worth more than many sparrows. Whoever acknowledges me before men, I will also acknowledge him before my Father in heaven. But whoever disowns me before men, I will disown him before My Father in heaven. Do not suppose that I came to bring peace to the earth. I do not come to bring peace, but a sword. For I have come to turn a man against his father, a daughter against her mother, a daughter-in-law against her mother-in-law– a man's enemies will be the members of his own household. Anyone who loves his father or mother more than me is not worthy of me; anyone who loves his son or daughter more than me is not worthy of me; and anyone who does not take his cross and follow me is not worthy of me. Whoever finds his life will lose it, and whoever loses his life for my sake will find it. He who receives you, receives me, and anyone who receives me, receives the one who sent me.Anyone who receives a prophet because he is a prophet will receive a prophet's reward, and anyone who receives a righteous man because he is a righteous man will receive a righteous man's reward. And if anyone gives even a cup of cold water to one of these little ones because he is my disciple, I tell you the truth, he will certainly not lose his reward.

Matthew 13 - Mark 6

Only in his hometown, among his relatives and in his own house is a prophet without honor.

JESUS' TRIBUTE TO JOHN
Matthew 11 - Luke 7

Go back and report to John what you hear and see: The blind receive sight, the lame walk, those who have leprosy are cured, the deaf hear, the dead are raised, and the good news is preached to the poor. Blessed is the man who does not fall away on account of me. What did you go out into the desert to see? A reed swayed by the wind? If not, what did you go out to see? A man dressed in fine clothes? No, those who wear fine clothes are in king's palaces! But what did you go out to see? A prophet? Yes, I tell you, and one who is more than a prophet. This is the one about whom it is written: 'Behold, I am sending my messenger ahead of you, who will prepare your way before you.' I tell you the truth, among those born of women there has not risen anyone greater than John the Baptist; yet he who is least in the kingdom of God is greater than he. From the days of John the Baptist until now, the kingdom of heaven has been forcefully advancing, and forceful men lay hold of it. For all the Prophets and the Law prophesied until John. And if you are willing to accept it, he is the Elijah who was to come. He who has ears, let him hear. To what can I compare this generation? They are like children sitting in the marketplace and calling out to the others, 'We played the flute for you, and you did not dance; we sang a song of mourning, and you did not mourn.' For John came neither eating nor drinking and they say, 'he has a demon.' The Son of Man comes eating and drinking, and they say, 'Here is a glutton and a drunkard, a friend of tax collectors and sinners.' But wisdom is proved right by her actions.

THE UNREPENTING CITIES
Matthew 11 - Luke 10

Woe to you, Chorazin! Woe to you, Bethsaida! If the miracles that were performed in you had been performed in Tyre and Sidon, they would have repented long ago in sackcloth and ashes. But I tell you, it will be more bearable for Tyre and Sidon on the day of judgement than for you. And you, Capernaum, will you be lifted up to the skies? No, you will go down to the depths. If miracles that were performed in you had been performed in Sodom, it would have remained to this day. But I tell you that it will be more bearable for Sodom on the day of judgement than for you. The one who listens to you listens to Me, and the one who rejects you rejects Me; but the one who rejects Me rejects the One who sent Me.

JESUS PRAISES THE FATHER
Matthew 11

I praise you, Father, Lord of heaven and earth, because you have hidden these things from the wise and learned, and revealed them to little children. Yes, Father, for this was your good pleasure. No one knows the Son except the Father, and no one knows the Father except the Son and those to whom the Son chooses to reveal Him. Come to Me, all you who are weary and burdened and I will give you rest. Take My yoke upon you and learn from me, for I am gentle and humble in heart, and you will find rest for your souls. For My yoke is easy and My burden is light.

JESUS, LORD OF THE SABBATH
Matthew 12 - Mark 3 - Luke 11

Every kingdom divided against itself will be ruined, and every city or household divided against itself will not stand. If Satan drives out Satan, he is divided against himself. How then can his kingdom stand? And if I drive out demons by Beelzebub, by whom do your people drive them out? So then, they will be your judges. But if I drive out demons by the Spirit (or "finger") of God, then the kingdom of God has come upon you. Or again, how can anyone enter a strong man's house and carry off his possessions unless he first ties up the strong man? Then he can rob his house. When a strong man, fully armed, guards his own house, his possessions are safe. But when someone stronger attacks and overpowers him, he takes away the armor in which the man trusted and divides up the spoils. He who is not with me is against me, and he who does not gather with me scatters. And so I tell you, every sin and blasphemy will be forgiven men, but the blasphemy against the Holy Spirit will not be forgiven. Anyone who speaks a word against the Son of Man will be forgiven, but anyone who speaks against the Holy Spirit will not be forgiven, either in this age or in the age to come. Make a tree good and its fruit will be good, or make a tree bad and its fruit will be bad, for a tree is recognized by its fruit. You brood of vipers, how can you who are evil say anything good? For out of the overflow of the heart the mouth speaks. The good man brings good things out of the good stored up in him, and the evil man brings evil things out of the evil stored up in him. But I tell you that men will have to give account on the day of judgement for every careless word they have spoken. For by your words you will be acquitted, and by your words you will be condemned. A wicked and adulterous generation asks for a miraculous sign! But none will be given it except the sign of the prophet Jonah. For as Jonah was three days and three nights in the belly of a huge fish, so the Son of Man will be three days and three nights in the heart of the earth.

The men of Ninevah will stand up at the judgement with this generation and condemn it; for they repented at the preaching of Jonah, and now one greater than Jonah is here. The Queen of the South will rise at the judgement with this generation and condemn it; for she came from the ends of the earth to listen to Solomon's wisdom, and now one greater than Solomon is here. When an evil spirit comes out of a man; it goes through arid places seeking rest and does not find it. Then it says, 'I will return to the house I left! When it arrives, it finds the house unoccupied, swept clean and put in order. Then it goes and takes with it seven other spirits more wicked than itself, and they go in and live there. And the final condition of that man is worse than the 1st. That is how it will be with this wicked generation.

JESUS' MOTHER AND BROTHER
Matthew 11 - Mark 3

Who are My mother and My brothers? Here are My mother and My brothers, for whoever does the will of My Father in heaven is My brother and sister and mother.

PARABLE OF SEEDS, YEAST, TREASURE, & FISHERMAN
Matthew 13 - Luke 8 - Mark 4

A farmer went out to sow his seed. As he was scattering seed, some fell along the path, and the birds came and ate it up. Some fell on rocky places, where it did not have much soil. It sprang up quickly, because the soil was shallow. But when the sun came up, the plants were scorched, and they withered because they had no root. Other seed fell among thorns, which grew up and choked the plants. Still other seed fell on good soil, where it produced a crop – a hundred, sixty or thirty times what was sown. He who has ears, let them hear. The knowledge of the secrets of the kingdom of heaven has been given to you, but not to them. Whoever has will be given more, and he will have an abundance. Whoever does not have, even what he has will be taken from him. This is why I speak to them in parables. Though seeing, they do not see, though hearing, they do not hear or understand. In them is fulfilled the prophecy of Isaiah: 'You will be ever hearing but never understanding you will be ever seeing but never perceiving. For this people's heart has become calloused; they hardly hear with their ears, and they closed their eyes, otherwise they might see with their eyes, hear with their ears, understand with their hearts and turn, and I would heal them.' But blessed are your ears, because they see, and your ears because they hear. For I tell you the truth, many prophets and righteous men longed to see what you see, but did not see, and hear what you hear but did not hear it.

Listen then to what the parable of the sower means: When anyone hears the message about the kingdom and does not understand it, the evil one comes and snatches away what was sown in his heart, so that they may not believe and be saved. This is the seed sown along the path. The one who received the seed that fell on rocky places is the man who hears the word and at once receives it with joy. But since he has no root, he lasts only a short time. When in time of testing, or trouble, or persecution comes because of the word, he quickly falls away. The one who received the seed that fell among the thorns is the man who hears the word, but the worries of this life and the deceitfulness of wealth and pleasure choke it, they do not mature and make it unfruitful. But the one who received the seed that fell on good soil stands for those with a noble and good heart, who hear the word, retain it, and by persevering produce a crop. He produces a crop yielding a hundred, sixty or thirty times what was sown.

The kingdom of heaven is like a man who sowed good seed in his field. But while everyone was sleeping, his enemy came and sowed weeds among the wheat, and went away. When the wheat sprouted and formed heads, then the weeds also appeared. The owner's servants came to him and said, 'Sir, didn't you sow good seed in your field? Where then did the weeds come from?'

'An enemy did this,' he replied. The servants asked him, 'Do you want us to go and pull them up?'

'No,' he answered, 'because while you are pulling the weeds, you may root up the wheat with them. Let both grow together until the harvest. At that time I will tell the harvesters: first collect the weeds and tie them in bundles to be burned; then gather the wheat and bring it into my barn.'

This is what the kingdom of God is like. A man scatters seed on the ground. Night and Day, whether he sleeps or gets up, the seed sprouts and grows, though he does not know how. All by itself the soil produces grain – first the stalk, then the head, then the full kernel in the head. As soon as the grain is ripe, he puts the sickle to it, because the harvest has come.

The kingdom of heaven is like a mustard seed, which a man took and planted in his field. Though it is the smallest of all your seeds, yet when it grows, it is the largest of garden plants and becomes a tree, so that the birds of the air come and perch in its branches.

The kingdom of heaven is like yeast that a woman took and mixed into a large amount of flour until it worked all through the dough.

The one who sowed the good seed is the Son of Man. The field is the world, and the good seed stands for the sons of the kingdom. The weeds are the sons of the evil one, and the enemy who sows them is the devil. The harvest is the end of the age, and the harvesters are the angels.

As the weeds are pulled up and burned in the fire, so it will be at the end of the age. The Son of Man will send out his angels, and they will be at the end of the age. The Son of Man will send out his angels, and they will weed out of his kingdom everything that causes sin and all who do evil. They will throw them into the fiery furnace, where there will be weeping and gnashing of teeth. Then the righteous will shine like the sun in the kingdom of their Father. He who has ears, let him hear. The kingdom of heaven is like treasure hidden in a field. When a man found it, he hid it again, and then in his joy went and sold all he had and bought that field. Again, the kingdom of heaven is like a merchant looking for fine pearls. When he found one of great value, he went away and sold everything he had and bought it. Once again, the kingdom of heaven is like a net that was let down into a lake and caught all kinds of fish. When it was full, the fisherman pulled it up on the shore. Then they sat down and collected the good fish in baskets, but threw the bad away. This is how it will be at the end of the age. The angels will come and separate the wicked from the righteous and throw them into the fiery furnace, where there will be weeping and gnashing of teeth. Have you understood all these things?
Therefore every teacher of the Law who has been instructed about the kingdom of heaven is like the owner of a house who brings out of his storeroom new treasures as well as old.

FEEDING THE 5,000 & JESUS WALKING ON WATER
Matthew 14 - Mark 6 - Luke 9 - John 6
Come with me by yourselves to a quiet place and get some rest. Where shall we buy bread for these people to eat? They need not go away. You give them something to eat. How many loaves do you have? Go and see. Bring them to me. Have them sit in groups of 50 each. Gather all the pieces that are leftover. Let nothing be wasted.
Take courage! It is I. Don't be afraid. Come. You of little faith, why did you doubt?

JESUS, THE BREAD OF LIFE
John 6
I tell you the truth, you are looking for me, not because you saw miraculous signs but because you ate the loaves and had your fill. Do not work for food that spoils, but for food that endures to eternal life, which the Son of Man will give you. On Him, God the Father has placed his seal of approval. The work of God is this: to believe in the one he has sent. I tell you the truth, it is not Moses who has given the bread from heaven, but it is My Father who gives you the true bread from heaven. For the bread of God is he who comes down from heaven and gives life to the world.

I am The Bread of Life. He who comes to me will never go hungry, and he who believes in me will never go thirsty. But as I told you, you have seen me and still you do not believe. All that the Father gives me will come to me, and whoever comes to me. I will never drive away. For I have come down from heaven not to do My will but to do the will of him who sent me. And this is the will of Him who sent me, that I shall lose none of all that He has given me, but raise them up at the last day. For My Father's will is that everyone who looks to the Son and believes in Him shall have eternal life, and I will raise Him up at the last day. Stop grumbling among yourselves, No one can come to me unless the Father who sent Him draws Him, and I will raise Him up at the last day. It is written in the prophets: 'They will all be taught by God.' Everyone who listens to the Father and learns from Him comes to Me. No one has seen the Father except the one who is from God; Only He has seen the Father. I tell you the truth, he who believes has everlasting life. I am the Bread of Life. Your forefathers ate the manna in the desert, yet they died. But here is the bread that comes down from heaven, which a man may eat and not die. I am the living bread that came down from heaven. If anyone eats of this bread, he will live forever. The bread is My flesh, which I will give for the life of the world. I tell you the truth, unless you eat the flesh of the Son of Man and drinks his blood, you have no life in you. Whoever eats My flesh and drinks My blood has eternal life, and I will raise Him up at the last day. For My flesh is real food and blood real drink. Whoever eats My flesh and drinks My blood remains in Me, and I in Him. Just as the living Father sent me and I live because of the Father, so the one who feeds on me will live because of me. This is the bread that came from heaven. Your forefathers ate manna and died, but he who feeds on this bread will live forever. Does this offend you? What if you see the Son of Man ascend to where he was before! The Spirit gives life; the flesh counts for nothing. The words I have spoken to you are spirit and they are life. Yet there are some of you who do not believe. This is why I told you that no one comes to me unless the Father has enables Him. You do not want to leave too, do you? Have I not chosen you, the Twelve? Yet one of you is a devil!

JESUS TEACHES AT THE FESTIVAL OF TABERNACLES
John 7
The right time for me has not yet come; for you at any time is right. The world cannot hate you, but it hates me because I testify that what it does is evil. You go to the feast, I am not yet going up to this feast, because for me the right time has not yet come. My teaching is not My own. It comes from Him who sent me. If anyone chooses to do God's will, he will find out whether My teaching comes from God or whether I speak on My own.

He who speaks on his own does so to gain honor for himself, but he who works for the honor of the one who sent him is a man of truth; there is nothing false about him. Has not Moses given you the Law? Yet not one of you keeps the Law. Why are you trying to kill me? I did one miracle; and you are all astonished. Yet because Moses gave you circumcision (though it came from the patriarchs), you circumcise a child on the Sabbath. Now if a child can be circumcised on the Sabbath so that the Law of Moses may not be broken, why are you angry with me for healing the whole man on the Sabbath? Stop judging by mere appearances, and make a righteous judgement. Yes, you know me, and you know where I am from. I am not here on My own, but who sent me is true. You do not know Him, but I know Him because I am from Him and He sent me. I am with you only for a short while, and then I go to the One who sent me. You will look for me, but you will not find me, and where I am, you cannot come. If anyone is thirsty, let him come to me and drink. Whoever believes in Me, as the Scriptures has said, streams of living water will flow from within him.

JESUS & THE WOMAN CAUGHT IN ADULTERY
John 8
If any one of you is without sin, let him be the first to throw the stone at her? Woman, where are they? Has no one condemned you? Then neither do I condemn you. Go now and leave your life of sin.

JESUS, THE LIGHT OF THE WORLD
John 8
I am the light of the world. Whoever follows me will never walk in darkness, but will have the light of life. Even if I testify on My own behalf, My testimony is valid, for I know where I came from and where I am going. But you have no idea where I came from or where I am going. You judge by human standards; I pass judgement on no one. But if I do judge, My decisions are right, because I am not alone. I stand with the Father, who sent me. In your own Law it is written that the testimony of two men is valid. I am one who testifies for Myself; My other witness is the Father who sent me. You do not know Me or My Father. If you knew me, you would know My father also. I am going away, and you will look for me, and you will die in your sin. Where I go, you cannot come. You are from below; I am from above. You are of this world, I am not of this world. You are of this world, I am not of this world. I told you that you would die in your sins; if you do not believe that I am the one, you will indeed die in your sins. Just what I have been claiming all along. I have much to say in judgement of you. But He who sent Me is reliable and what I have heard from Him I tell the world.

When you have lifted up the Son of Man, then you will know that I am the one I claim to be, and that I do nothing on My own but speak just what the Father has taught me. The one who sent me is with me; He has not left me alone, for I always do what pleases Him. If you hold to My teaching, you are truly My disciples. Then you will know the truth, everyone who sins is a slave to sin. Now a slave has no permanent place in the family, but a son belongs to it forever. So if the Son sets you free, you will be free indeed. I know you are Abraham's descendants. Yet you are ready to kill me, because you have no room for My word. I am telling you what I have seen in the Father's presence, and you do what you have heard from your father. If you were Abraham's children, then you would do the things Abraham did. As it is, you are determined to kill me, a man who has told you the truth that I heard from God. Abraham did not do such things. You are doing the things your own father does. If God were your Father, you would love me, for I came from God and now am here. I have not come on My own; but he who sent me. Why is My language not clear to you? Because you are unable to hear what I say. You belong to your Father, the devil, and you want to carry out your Father's desire. He was a murderer from the beginning, not holding to the truth, for there is no truth in him. When he lies, he speaks his native language, for he is a liar and the father of lies. Yet because I tell the truth, you do not believe me! Can any of you prove me guilty of sins? If I am telling the truth, why don't you believe me? He who belongs to God hears what God says. The reason you do not hear is that you do not belong to God. I am not possessed by a demon, but I honor My Father and you dishonor me. I am not seeking glory for Myself; but there is one who seeks it, and he is the judge. I tell you the truth, if anyone keeps My word, he will never see death. If I glorify Myself, My glory means nothing. My Father, whom you claim as your God, is the one who glorifies me. Though you do not know Him, I know Him. If I said I did not, I would be as a liar like you, but I do know Him and keep His word. Your Father Abraham rejoiced at the thought of seeing My day; he saw it and was glad. I tell you the truth, before Abraham was born, I am!

JESUS & THE BLIND MAN
Matthew 20 - Mark 10 - Luke 18 - John 9
Call him. What do you want me to do for you?
Neither this man nor his parents sinned, but this happened so that the work of God might be displayed in his life. As long as it is day, we must do the work of Him who sent me. Night is coming, when no one can work. While I am in the world, I am the light of the world. Go, receive your sight, your faith has healed you. Go, wash in the pool of Siloam. Do you believe in the Son of Man. You have now seen Him; in fact, he is the one speaking with you.

For judgement I have come into this world, so that the blind will see and those who see will become blind. If you were blind, you would not be guilty of sin; but now that you claim to see, your guilt remains.

TRADITION AND COMMANDMENTS
Matthew 15 - Mark 7

And why do you break the command of God for the sake of tradition? For God said, 'Honor your father and mother' and 'any one who curses his father or mother must be put to death.' But you say that if a man says to his father and mother, 'Whatever help you might otherwise have received from me is a gift devoted to God.' He is not to 'honor his father' with it. Thus you nullify the word of God for the sake of your tradition. You hypocrites! Isaiah was right when he prophesied about you: 'These people honor me with their lips, but their hearts are far from me. They worship me in vain; their teachings are but rules taught by men.' You have let go of the commands of God and are holding on to the traditions of men. Listen to me, everyone, and understand this. Nothing outside a man can make him unclean by going into him. Rather, it is what comes out of a man that makes him unclean. Every plant that My heavenly Father has not planted will be pulled up by the roots. Leave them; they are blind guides. If a blind man leads a blind man, both will fall into a pit.

Are you still so dull? Don't you see that whatever enters the mouth comes from the heart and then out of the body? But the things that come out of the mouth come from the heart, and these make a man unclean. For out of heart come evil thoughts, greed, murder, malice, adultery, envy, sexual immorality, arrogance, theft, false testimony, folly, slander. These are what makes a man unclean, but eating with unwashed hands does not make him unclean.

JESUS & THE CANAANITE (SYROPHOENICIAN) WOMAN
Matthew 15 - Mark 7

I was only sent to the lost sheep of Israel. First let the children eat all they want, for it is not right to take the children's bread and toss it to their dogs. Woman, you have great faith! Your request is granted. For such a reply, you may go; the demon has left your daughter.

JESUS & THE 4,000
Matthew 15 - Mark 6

I have compassion for these people; they have already been with me 3 days and have nothing to eat. If I send them home hungry, they will collapse on the way, because some of them have come a long distance. How many loaves do you have?

VARIOUS MIRACLES
Mark 7-8 - Luke 7
[to the mute man] Ephphatha (be opened)!
[to the blind man] Do you see anything? Don't go into the village.
[to the widow] Don't cry
[to her son] Young man, I say to you get up!

THE YEAST OF THE PHARISEES
Matthew 16 - Mark 8 - Luke 12
When evening comes, you say, 'it will be fair weather, for the sky is red,' and in the morning 'today it will be stormy, for the sky is red and overcast.' You know how to interpret the appearance of the sky, but you cannot interpret the signs of the times. A wicked and adulterous generation looks for a miraculous sign, but none will be given except for the sign of Jonah. Watch out and beware of the yeast of the Pharisees and Sudducees. You men of little faith, why are you discussing among yourselves the fact that you have no bread? Do you not yet understand nor remember the five loaves for the five thousand, and how many basketfuls you gathered? Nor the seven loaves of the four thousand, and how many basketfuls you picked up? How is it that you do not understand that I did not speak to you about bread? But beware of the yeast of the Pharisees and Sudducees.

PETER'S EXALTATION AND REBUKE
Matthew 16 - Mark 8 - Luke 9
WHo do people say the Son of Man is? Who do the crowds say that I am? But what about you? Who do you say that I am?
Blessed are you Simon, son of Jonah, for this was not revealed to you by man, but by My Father in heaven. And I tell you that you are Peter, and on this rock I will build My church, and the gates of Hades will not overcome it. I will give you the keys of the kingdom of heaven; whatever you bind on earth will be bound in heaven, and whatever you loose on earth will be loosed in heaven.
The Son of Man must suffer many things and be rejected by the elders, chief priests and teachers of the Law, and he must be killed and on the third day be raised to life.
Get behind me Satan! You are a stumbling block to me; you do not have in mind the things of God, but the things of men. If anyone would come after me, he must deny himself and take up his cross and follow me. For whoever wants to save his life will lose it, but whoever loses his life for me will find it. What good will it be for a man if he gains the whole world, yet forfeits his soul?

For the Son of Man is going to come in His Father's glory with his angels, and then he will reward each person according to what he has done. I tell you the truth, some who are standing here will not taste death before they see the Son of Man coming in his kingdom. If anyone is ashamed of My words, the Son of Man will be ashamed of him when He comes in His glory and the glory of the Father and His holy angels.

MOUNT OF TRANSFIGURATION & THE VALLEY
Matthew 17 - Mark 9 - Luke 9
THIS IS MY SON, WHOM I HAVE CHOSEN, WHOM I LOVE, LISTEN TO HIM.
Get up, don't be afraid. Don't tell anyone what you have seen, until the Son of Man has been raised from the dead. To be sure, Elijah comes and will restore all things. But I tell you, Elijah has already come, and they did not recognize him, but have done to him everything they wished. In the same way, the Son of Man is going to suffer at their hands.
What are you arguing with them about? O unbelieving and perverse generation, how long shall I stay with you? How long shall I put up with you? How long has he been like this?,
'If you can'? Everything is possible for him who believes.
You deaf and mute spirit, I command you, come out of him and never enter him again. This kind only comes out by prayer and fasting. Because you have so little faith. I tell you the truth, if you have faith as small as a mustard seed, you can say to this mountain, 'move from here to there' and it will move. Nothing will be impossible for you. Listen carefully to what I am about to tell you; The Son of Man is going to be betrayed into the hands of men. They will kill Him, and on the third day he will be raised to life.

THE TEMPLE TAX
Matthew 17
What do you think, Simon? From whom do the kings of the earth collect duty and taxes– from their own sons or from others? The sons are exempt, but so that we may not offend them, go to the lake and throw out your line. Take the first fish and you catch; open his mouth and you will find a 4-darachma coin. Take it and give it to them for My tax and yours.

RANK & WARNINGS
Matthew 18 - Mark 9 - Luke 9
What were you arguing about on the road? If anyone wants to be first, he must be the very last, and servant of all. I tell you the truth, unless you change and become like little children, you will never enter the kingdom of heaven. Therefore, whoever humbles himself like this child is the greatest in the kingdom of heaven. And whoever welcomes a little child like this in My name, welcomes Me. And whoever welcomes Me welcomes the One who sent Me. For he who is least among you all– is the greatest. Do not hinder him, for there is no one who will perform a miracle in My name, and be able soon afterward to speak evil of Me. For the one who is not against us is for us. For whoever gives you a cup of water to drink because of your name as followers of Christ, truly I say to you, he shall by no means lose his reward. But if anyone causes one of these little ones to sin, it would be better for him to have a large millstone hung around his neck and to be drowned in the depths of the sea. Woe to the world because of the things that cause people to sin! Such things must come, but woe to that man through whom they come! If your hand or foot causes you to sin, cut it off and throw it away. It is better for you to enter life maimed or crippled than to have two hands or two feet and be thrown into eternal fire. And if your eye causes you to sin, gouge it out and throw it away. It is better for you to enter life with one eye than to have two eyes and be thrown into the gehenna of fire, where their worm does not die, and the fire is not extinguished. For everyone is salted with fire. Salt is good; but if the salt becomes unsalty, with what will you make it salty again? Have salt in yourselves, and be at peace with one another.
Foxes have holes and birds of the air have nests, but the Son of Man has no place to lay his head. Follow Me. Let the dead bury their own dead, but you go and proclaim the kingdom of God. No one who puts his hand to the plow and looks back is fit for service in the kingdom of God.

JESUS, THE GATE & THE GOOD SHEPHERD
Matthew 18 - John 10
See that you do not look down on one of these little ones. For I tell you that their angels in heaven always see the face of My Father in heaven. What do you think? If a man owns a hundred sheep, and one of them wanders away, will he not leave the ninety-nine on the hills and go to look for the one that wandered off? And if he find its, I tell you the truth, he is happier about that one sheep than about the ninety-nine that did not wander off. In the same way, your Father in heaven is not will that any of these little ones should be lost.

I tell you the truth, the man who does not enter the sheep pen by the gate, but climbs in by some other way, is a thief and a robber. The man who enters by the gate is the shepherd of his sheep. The watchman opens the gate for him, and the sheep listen to his voice. He calls his own sheep by name and leads them out. When he has brought out all his own, he goes on ahead of them, and the sheep follow him because they know his voice. But they will never follow a stranger; in fact, they will run away from him because they do not recognize a stranger's voice. I tell you the truth, I am the gate for the sheep. All whoever came before Me were thieves and robbers, but the sheep did not listen to them. I am the gate; whoever enters through me will be saved. He will come in and go out, and find pasture. The thief comes only to steal and kill and destroy; I have come that they may have life, and have it to the full. I am the good shepherd. The good shepherd lays down his life for the sheep. The hired hand is not the shepherd who owns the sheep, so when he sees the wolf coming, he abandons the sheep and runs away. Then the wolf attacks the flock and scatters it. The man runs away because he is a hired hand and cares nothing for the sheep. I am the good shepherd; I know My sheep and My sheep know me– just as the father knows me and I know the father– and I lay down My life for the sheep. I have other sheep that are not of this sheep pen. I must bring them also. They too will listen to My voice, and there shall be one flock and one shepherd. The reason My Father loves Me is that I lay down My life– only to take it up again. No one takes it from me, but I lay it down and authority to take it up again. This command I received from My Father.

I did tell you, but you do not believe. The miracles I do in My Father's name speak for me, but you do not believe because you are not my sheep. My sheep listen to My voice; I know them and they follow me. I give them eternal life, and they shall never perish; no one can snatch out of My hand. My Father, who has given them to me, is greater than all; no one can snatch them out of My Father's hand. I and the Father are one. I have shown you many great miracles from the Father, for which of these do you stone me?

It is written in your Law, 'I have said you are gods? If he called them 'gods,' to whom the word of God came– and the Scripture cannot be broken– what about the one whom the Father set apart as His very own and sent into the world? Why then do you accuse me of blasphemy because I said 'I am God's Son'? But if I do it, even though you do not believe me, believe the miracles, that you may know and understand that the Father is in Me; and I in the Father.

CONFRONTATION, PRAYER, FORGIVENESS
Matthew 18
Now if your brother sins against you go and show him his fault, just between the two of you. If he listens to you, you have won your brother over. But if he will not listen, take one or two others along, so that 'every matter may be established by the testimony of two or three witnesses. If he refuses to listen to them, tell it to the church; and if he refuses to listen even to the church, treat him as you would a pagan or a tax collector. I tell you the truth, whatever you bind on earth will be bound in heaven and whatever you loose on earth will be loosed in heaven. Again, I tell you that if two of you on earth agree about anything you ask for, it will be done for you by My Father in heaven. For where two or more come together in My name, there am I with them. I do not say to you, forgive them up to seven times, but up to seventy-seven times. For this reason the kingdom of heaven is like a king who wanted to settle accounts with his slaves. And when he had begun to settle them, one who owed him ten thousand talents was brought to him. But since he did not have the means to repay, his master ordered that he and his wife and his children and all that he had be sold to repay the debt. The slave fell to the ground and prostrated himself before him, saying, 'Have patience with me and I will repay you everything.' And the master of that slave felt compassion, and he released him and forgave him the debt. But that slave went out and found one of his fellow slaves who owed him a hundred denarii; and he seized him and began to choke him, saying, 'Pay back what you owe!' So his fellow slave fell to the ground and began to plead with him, saying, 'Have patience with me and I will repay you.' But he was unwilling, and went and threw him in prison until he would pay back what was owed. So when his fellow slaves saw what had happened, they were deeply grieved and came and reported to their master all that had happened. Then summoning him, his master said to him, 'You wicked slave, I forgave you all that debt because you pleaded with me. Should you not also have had mercy on your fellow slave, in the same way I had mercy on you?' And his master, moved with anger, handed him over to the torturers until he would repay all that was owed him. My heavenly Father will also do the same to you, if each of you does not forgive his brother from your heart.

JESUS SENDS OUT THE 72
Luke 10
The harvest is plentiful, but the workers are few. Ask the Lord of the harvest, therefore, to send out workers in his harvest field. Go! I am sending you out like lambs among wolves. Do not take a purse or bag or sandals; and do not greet anyone on the road. When you enter a house, first say, 'Peace to this house.'

If a man of peace is there, your peace will rest on him; if not, it will return to you. Stay in that house, eating and drinking whatever they give you, for the worker deserves his wages. Do not move around from house to house. When you enter a town and are welcomed, eat what is set before you. Heal the sick who are there and tell them, 'the kingdom of God is near you.' But when you enter a town and are not welcomed, go into its streets and say 'Even the dust of your town that sticks to our feet we wipe off against you. Yet be sure of this, the kingdom of God is near.' I tell you, it will be more bearable on that day for Sodom than for that town. Woe to you, Korazin! Woe to you, Bethsaida! For if the miracles that were performed in you had been performed in Tyre and Sidon, they would have repented long ago, sitting in sackcloth and ashes. But it will be more bearable for Tyre and Sidon at the judgement than for you. And you, Capernaum, will you be lifted up to the skies? No, you will go down to the depths. He who listens to you, listens to Me; he who rejects you, rejects Me; but he who rejects Me, rejects Him who sent Me. I saw Satan fall from heaven like lightning. I have you authority to trample on snakes and scorpions and to overcome all the power of the enemy; nothing will harm you. However, do not rejoice that the spirits submit to you, but rejoice that your names are written in heaven. I praise you, Father, Lord of heaven and earth, because you have hidden these things from the wise and learned, and revealed them to little children. Yes, Father, for this was your good pleasure. All things have been committed to Me by My Father. No one knows who the Son is except the Father, and no one knows who the Father is except the Son and those to whom the Son chooses to reveal Him. Blessed are the eyes that see what you see. For I tell you that many prophets and kings wanted to see what you see but did not see it, and to hear what you hear but did not hear it.

PARABLE OF THE GOOD SAMARITAN
Luke 10
What is written in the Law? How do you read it?
You have answered correctly, do this and you will live. A man was going down from Jerusalem to Jericho, when he fell into the hands of robbers. They stripped him of his clothes, beat him and went away, leaving him half dead. A priest happened to be going down the same road, and when he saw the man, he passed by on the side. So too, a Levite, when he came to the place and saw him, passed by the other side of the ride. But a Samaritan, as he traveled, came where the man was; and when he saw him, he took pity on him. He went to him and bandaged his wounds, pouring on oil and wine. Then he put the man on his own donkey, took him to an inn and took care of him. The next day he took out two silver coins and gave them to the innkeeper.

'Look after him,' he said, 'and when I return, I will reimburse you for any extra expense you may have.' Which of these three do you think was a neighbor to the man who fell into the hands of robbers? Go and do likewise.

DIVORCE & EUNUCHS
Matthew 19 - Mark 10

What did Moses command you?

Haven't you read, that at the beginning the Creator 'made them male and female, for this reason a man will leave his father and mother and be united to his wife, and the two will become one flesh'? So they are no longer two, but one. Therefore what God has joined together, let man not separate. Moses permitted you to divorce your wives because your hearts were hard. But it was not this way from the beginning. I tell you that anyone who divorces his wife, except for marital unfaithfulness, and marries another woman commits adultery against her. And if she divorces her husband and marries another man, she commits adultery.

Not everyone can accept this word, but only those to whom it has been given. For some are eunuchs because they are born that way; others were made that way by men; and others have renounced marriage because of the kingdom of heaven. The one who can accept this, should accept this.

CHILDREN, THE YOUNG RICH RULER & THE DISCIPLES' REWARD
Matthew 19 - Mark 10 - Luke 18

Let the little children come to me and do not hinder them. For the kingdom of God belongs to such as these. I tell you the truth, anyone who will not receive the kingdom of God like a little child will never enter it.

Why do you call me good? No one is good– except God alone. There is only One who is good, if you want to enter life, obey the commandments.

You know the commandments: 'Do not murder, do not commit adultery, do not steal, do not give false testimony, honor your father and mother,' and 'you shall love your neighbor as yourself.'

One thing you lack. If you want to be perfect, go, sell all your possessions and everything you have, give it to the poor, and you will have treasure in heaven. Then come & follow me. I tell you the truth, how hard it is for the rich to enter the kingdom of God! Again I tell you, children, how hard it is to enter the kingdom of God! It is easier for a camel to go through the eye of a needle than for a rich man to enter the kingdom of God. With man this is impossible, but with God all things are possible.

I tell you the truth, at the renewal of all things, when the Son of Man sits on His glorious throne, you who have followed me will also sit on 12 thrones, judging the 12 tribes of Israel. And everyone who has left home or brothers or sisters or mother or father or children or fields for Me and the gospel will receive 100x as much in this present age and in the age to come, eternal life. But many who are first will be last, and many who are last will be first.

SERMON ON THE PLAIN
Luke 12

Be on your guard against the yeast of the Pharisees, which is hypocrisy. There is nothing concealed that will not be disclosed, or hidden that will not be made known. What you have said in the dark will be heard in the daylight, and what you have whispered in the ear in the inner rooms will be proclaimed from the roofs. I tell you, My friend, do not be afraid of those who kill the body and after that can do no more. But I will show you whom you should fear: Fear Him who, after the killing of the body has power to throw you into gehenna. Yes, I tell you, fear Him. Are not five sparrows sold for two assaria? Yet not one of them is forgotten by God. Indeed the very hairs of your head are all numbered. Don't be afraid; you are worth more than many sparrows. I tell you, whoever acknowledges me before men, the Son of Man will acknowledge him before the angels of God. But he who disowns me before men will be disowned before the angels of God. And everyone who speaks a word against the Son of Man will be forgiven, but anyone who blasphemes against the Holy Spirit will not be forgiven. When you are brought before synagogues, rulers and authorities, do not worry about how you will defend yourselves or what you will say for the Holy Spirit will teach you at the time what you should say.

Man, who appointed me a judge or an arbiter between? Watch out! Be on your guard against all kinds of greed; a man's life does not consist in the abundance of his possessions. The ground of a certain rich man produced a good crop. He thought to himself, 'What shall I do? I have no place to store my crops.' Then he said, 'This is what I'll do, I will tear down my barns and build bigger ones, and there I will store all my grain and my goods. And I'll say to myself 'You have plenty of good things laid up for many years. Take life easy; eat, drink, and be merry." But God said, 'You fool! This very night your soul is demanded of you. Then who will get what you have prepared for yourself?' This is how it will be with anyone who stores up things for himself, but is not rich toward God. Therefore I tell you, do not worry about your life, what you will eat; or about your body, what you will wear. Life is more than food, and the body more than clothes. Consider the ravens; they do not sow or reap, they have no storeroom or barn; yet God feeds them.

And how much more valuable you are than birds! Who of you by worrying can add a single hour to his life? Since you cannot do this very little thing, why do you worry about the rest? Consider how the lilies grow. They do not labor or spin. Yet I tell you, not even Solomon in all his splendor was dressed like one of these. If that is how God clothes the grass of the field, which is here today, and tomorrow is thrown into the fire, how much more will he clothe you, O you of little faith! And do not set your heart on what you will eat or drink; do not worry about it. For the pagan world runs after all such things, and your Father knows that you need them. But seek his kingdom, and these things will be given to you as well! Do not be afraid, little flock, for your Father has been pleased to give you the kingdom. Sell your possessions and give to the poor. Provide purses for yourselves that will not wear out, a treasure in heaven that will not be exhausted, where no thief comes near and no moth destroys. For where your treasure is, there your heart will be also. Be dressed and ready for service and keep your lamps burning, like men waiting for their master to return from a wedding banquet, so that when he comes and knocks they can immediately open the door for him. It will be good for those servants whose master finds them watching when he comes. I tell you the truth, he will dress himself to serve, will have them recline at the table and will come and wait on them. It will be good for those servants whose master finds them watching when he comes. I tell you the truth, he will dress himself to serve, will have them recline at the table and he will come and wait on them. It will be good for those servants whose master finds them ready, even if he comes in the second or third watch of the night. But understand this: If the owner of the house had known at what hour the thief was coming, he would not have let his house be broken into. You must also be ready, because the Son of Man will come at an hour when you do not expect Him. Who then is the faithful and wise manager, whom the master put in charge of his servants to give them their food allowance at the proper time? It will be good for that servant whom the master finds doing so when he returns. I tell you the truth, he will put him in charge of all his possessions. But suppose the servant says to himself, 'My master is taking a long time in coming.' and he then begins to beat the menservants and mainservants and to eat and drink and get drunk. The master of that servant will come on a day when he does not expect him and at an hour he is not aware of. He will cut him to pieces and assign him a place with the unbelievers. That servant who knows his master's will and does not get ready or does not do what his master wants will be beaten with many blows. But the one who does not know and does things deserving punishment will be beaten with few blows.

From everyone who has been given much, much will be demanded; and from the one who has been entrusted with much, much more will be asked. I have come to bring fire on the earth, and how I wish it were already kindled! But I have a baptism to undergo, and how distressed I am until it is completed! Do you think I came to bring peace on earth? No, I tell you, but division. From now on there will be five in one family divided against each other, three against two and two against three. They will be divided, father against son and son against father, mother against daughter and daughter against mother, mother-in-law against daughter-in-law and daughter-in-law against mother-in-law. When you see a cloud rising in the west, immediately you say, 'it is going to rain,' and it does. And when the south wind blows you say, 'it's going to be hot,' and it is! Hypocrites! You know how to interpret the appearance of the earth and the sky. How is it that you don't know how to interpret this present time? Why don't you judge for yourselves what is right? As you are going with your adversary to the magistrate, try hard to be reconciled to him on the way, or he may drag you to the judge, and the judge turns you over to the officer, and the officer throws you into prison. I tell you, you will not get out until you paid the last lepton.

PREACHING & HEALING
Luke 13
Do you think these Galileans were worse sinners than all the other Galileans because they suffered this way? I tell you, no! But unless you repent, you too will all perish. Or those eighteen who died when the tower of Siloam fell on them– do you think they were more guilty than all the others living in Jerusalem? I tell you, no! But unless you repent, you too will all perish! A man had a fig tree planted in his vineyard and he went to look for fruit on it, but did not find any. So he said to the man who took care of the vineyard, 'For three years now I've been coming to look for fruit on this fig tree and haven't found any. Cut it down! Why should it use up the soil?'
'Sir,' the man replied, 'leave it alone for one more year, and I'll dig around it and fertilize it. If it bears fruit next year, fine! If not, then cut it down.'
Woman, you are set free from your infirmity.
You hypocrites! Doesn't each of you on the Sabbath untie his ox or donkey from the stall and lead it out to give it water? Then should not this woman, a daughter of Abraham, whom Satan has kept bound for eighteen long years, be set free on the Sabbath day from what bound her? What is the kingdom of God like? What shall I compare it to? It is like a mustard seed, which a man took and planted in his garden. It grew and the birds of the air perched in its branches.

What shall I compare the kingdom of God to? It is like yeast that a woman took and mixed into a large amount of flour until it worked all through the dough. Make every effort to enter through the narrow door. I tell you, because many will try to enter and will not be able to. Once the owner of the house gets up and closes the door, you will stand outside knocking and pleading, 'Sir, open the door for us.' but he will answer, 'I don't know you or where you come from.' Then you will say, 'We ate and drank with you, and you taught in our streets.' But he will reply, 'I don't know you or where you come from. Away from me, all you evildoers!' There will be weeping and gnashing of teeth, when you see Abraham, Isaac, and Jacob, and all the prophets in the kingdom of God, but you yourselves will be thrown out. People will come from the east and west and north and south, and will take their places at the feast of the kingdom of God. Indeed there are those who are last who will be first, and first who will be last.

Go and tell that fox [Herod], 'I will drive out demons and heal people today and tomorrow, and on the third day I will reach my goal.' In any case, I must keep going today and tomorrow and the next day– for surely no prophet can die outside Jerusalem! O Jerusalem, Jerusalem, you who kill the prophets and stone those sent to you, how often I longed to gather your children together, as a hen gathers her chicks under her wings, but you were not willing! Look, your house is left to you desolate, I tell you, you will not see me again until you say, 'Blessed is he who comes in the name of the Lord.'

PARABLES OF THE BANQUETS & INTENSITY OF DISCIPLESHIP
Luke 14

Is it lawful to heal on the Sabbath or not? If one of you has a son or an ox that falls into a well on the Sabbath day, will you not immediately pull him out? When someone invites you to a wedding feast, do not take the place of honor, for a person more distinguished than you may have been invited. If so, the host who invited both of you will come and say to you, 'Give this man your seat.' Then, humiliated, you will have to take the least important seat. But when you are invited, take the lowest place, so that when your host comes, he will say to you, 'Friend, move up to a better place.' Then you will be honored in the presence of all your fellow guests. For everyone who exalts himself will be humbled. And he who humbles himself will be exalted. When you give a luncheon or dinner, do not invite your friends, your brothers or relatives, or your rich neighbors; if you do, they may invite you back and so you will be repaid. But when you give a banquet, invite the poor, the crippled, the lame, the blind, and you will be blessed. Although they cannot repay you, you will be repaid at the resurrection of the righteous.

A certain man was preparing a great banquet and invited many guests. At the time of the banquet he sent his servant to tell those who had been invited, 'Come, for everything is now ready.' But they alike began to make excuses. The first said, 'I have just bought five yokes of oxen, and I'm on my way to try them out. Please excuse me.' Still another said, 'I just got married, so I can't come.' The servant came and reported this to his master. Then the owner of the house became angry and ordered his servant, 'Go out quickly into the streets and alleys of the town and bring in the poor, the crippled, the blind and the lame.' 'Sir,' the servant said, 'What you ordered has been done, but there is still room.' Then the master told his servants, 'Go out to the roads and country lanes and make them come in, so that my house will be full. I tell you, not one of those men who were invited will get a taste of my banquet. If anyone comes to me and does not hate his father and mother, his wife and children, his brothers and sisters— yes, even his own life— he cannot be my disciple. And anyone who does not carry his cross and follow me cannot be my disciple. Suppose one of you wants to build a tower. Will he not first sit down and estimate the cost to see if he has enough money to complete it? For if he lays the foundation and is not able to finish it, everyone who sees it will ridicule him, saying 'This fellow began to build and was not able to finish.' Or suppose a king is about to go to war against another king. Will he not first sit down and consider whether he is able with 10,000 men to oppose the one coming against him with 20,000? If he is not able, he will send a delegation while the other is still a long way off and will ask for terms of peace. In the same way, any of you who does not give up everything he has cannot be my disciple. Salt is good, but if it loses its saltiness, how can it be made salty again? It is fit neither for soil nor for the manure piles; it is thrown out. He who has ears to hear, let him hear.

LOST PARABLES
Luke 15
Suppose one of you has a hundred sheep and loses one of them. Does he not leave the ninety-nine in the open country and go after the lost sheep until he finds it? And when he finds it, he joyfully puts it on his shoulders and goes home. Then he calls his friends and neighbors together and says, 'Rejoice with me; I have found my lost sheep.' I tell you that in the same way there will be more rejoicing in heaven over one sinner who repents than over ninety-nine righteous persons who do not need to repent.
Or suppose a woman has 10 silver coins and loses one. Does she not light a lamp, sweep the house and search carefully until she finds it? And when she finds it, she calls her friends and neighbors together and says

'Rejoice with me; I have found my lost coin.' In the same way I tell you, there is rejoicing in the presence of the angels of God over one sinner who repents. There was a man who had two sons. The younger one said to his father, 'Father, give me my share of the estate.' So he divided his property between them. Not long after that, the younger son got together all he had, set off for a distant country and there squandered his wealth on wild living. After he had spent everything, there was a severe famine in that whole country, and he began to be in need. So he went and hired himself out to a citizen of that country, who sent him to his fields to feed pigs. He longed to fill his stomach with the pods that the pigs were eating, but no one gave him anything. When he came to his senses, he said, 'How many of y father's hired men have food to spare, and here I am starving to death! I will set out and go back to my father and say to him: Father, I have sinned against heaven and against you. I am no longer worthy to be called your son; make me like one of your hired men.' So he got up and went to his father. But while he was still a long way off, his father saw him and was filled with compassion for him; he ran to his son, threw his arms around him and kissed him. The son said to him, 'Father, I have sinned against heaven and against you. I am no longer worthy to be called your son.'

But the Father said to his servants, 'Quick! Bring the best robe and put it on him. Put a ring on his finger and sandals on his feet. Bring the fattened calf and kill it. Let's have a feast and celebrate. For this son of mine was dead and is alive again; he was lost and is found.' So they began to celebrate. Meanwhile, the older son was in the field. When he came near the house, he heard music and dancing. So he called one of the servants and asked him what was going on. 'Your brother has come,' he replied, 'and your father has killed the fattened calf because he has him back safe and sound.' The older brother became angry and refused to go in. So his father went out and pleaded with him. But he answered his father, 'Look! All these years I've been slaving for you and never disobeyed your orders. Yet you never gave me even a young goat so I could celebrate with my friends. But when this son of yours who has squandered your property with prostitutes comes home, you kill the fattened calf for him! 'My son,' the father said, 'You are always with me, and everything I have is yours. But we had to celebrate and be glad, because this brother of yours was dead and is alive again; he was lost and is found.'

THE UNRIGHTEOUS MANAGER, THE RICH MAN & LAZARUS
Luke 16

There was a rich man whose manager was accused of wasting his possessions. So he called him in and asked him, 'What is this I hear about you?

Give an account of your management, because you cannot be manager any longer.' The manager said to himself, 'What shall I do now? My master is taking away my job. I'm not strong enough to dig, and I'm ashamed to beg– I know what I'll do so that, when I lose my job here, people will welcome me into their houses.' So he called in each one of his master's debtors. He asked the first, 'How much do you owe my master?'

'Nine hundred gallons of olive oil,' he replied. The manager told him, 'Take your bill, sit down quickly, and make it four hundred and fifty.' Then he asked the second, 'And how much do you owe?'

A thousand bushels of wheat,' he replied. He told him, 'Take your bill and make it eight hundred.' The master commended the dishonest manager because he acted shrewdly. For the people of this world are more shrewd dealing with their own kind than are the people of the light. I tell you, use worldly wealth to gain friends for yourselves, so that when it is gone, you will be welcomed into eternal dwellings. Whoever can be trusted with very little can also be trusted with much, and whoever is dishonest with very little will also be dishonest with much. So if you have not been trustworthy in handling worldly wealth, who will trust you with true riches? And if you have not been trustworthy with someone else's property, who will give you property of your own? No one can serve two masters. Either you will hate the one and love the other, or you will be devoted to the one and despise the other. You cannot serve both God and money.

You are the ones who justify yourselves in the eyes of others, but God knows your hearts. What people value highly is detestable in God's sight. The Law and the Prophets were proclaimed until John. Since that time, the good news of the kingdom of God is being preached, and everyone is forcing their way into it. It is easier for heaven and earth to disappear than for the least stroke of a pen to drop out of the Law. Anyone who divorces his wife and marries another woman commits adultery, and the man who marries a divorced woman commits adultery. There was a rich man who was dressed in purple and fine linen and lived in luxury every day. At his gate was laid a beggar named Lazarus, covered with sores and longing to eat what fell from the rich man's table. Even the dogs came and licked his sores.

The time came when the beggar died and the angels carried him to Abraham's side. The rich man also died and was buried. In Hades, where he was in torment, he looked up and saw Abraham far away, with Lazarus by his side. So he called to him, 'Father Abraham, have pity on me and send Lazarus to dip the tip of his finger in water and cool my tongue, because I am in agony in this fire.'

But Abraham replied, 'Son, remember that in your lifetime you received your good things, while Lazarus received bad things, but now he is comforted here and you

are in agony. And besides all this, between us and you a great chasm has been set in place, so that those who want to go from here to you cannot, nor can anyone cross over from there to us.'

He answered, 'Then I beg you, father, send Lazarus to my family, for I have five brothers. Let him warn them, so that they will not also come to this place of torment.'

Abraham replied, 'They have Moses and the Prophets; let them listen to them.'

'No, father Abraham,' he said, 'but if someone from the dead goes to them, they will repent.'

He said to him, 'If they do not listen to Moses and the Prophets, they will not be convinced even if someone rises from the dead.'

INSTRUCTIONS & TEN LEPERS
Luke 17

Things that cause people to sin are bound to come, but woe to that person through whom they come. It would be better for him to be thrown into the sea with a millstone tied around his neck than for him to cause one of these little ones to sin. So watch yourselves. If your brother sins, rebuke him, and if he repents, forgive him. If he sins against you seven times in a day and seven times comes back to you and says, 'I repent,' forgive him. If you have faith as small as a mustard seed, you can say to this mulberry tree, 'be uprooted and planted in the sea,' and it will obey you. Suppose one of you had a servant plowing or looking after the sheep. Would he say to the servant when he comes in from the field, 'Come along now and sit down to eat'? Would he say to the servant when he comes in from the field, 'Come along now and sit down to eat'? Would he not rather say, 'Prepare my supper, get yourself ready and wait on me while I eat and drink; after that you may eat and drink'? Would he thank the servant because he did what he was told to do? So you also, when you have done everything you were told to do, should say, 'We are unworthy servants; we have only done our duty.'

'Go, show yourselves to the priests.'

'Were not all ten cleansed? Where are the other nine? Was no one found to return and give praise to God except this foreigner? Rise and go; your faith has made you well.'

THE SECOND COMING
Luke 17

The kingdom of God does not come with your careful observation, nor will people say, 'Here it is,' or 'There it is,' because the kingdom of God is within you. The time is coming when you will long to see one of the days of the Son of Man, but

you will not see it. Men will tell you, 'There he is!' or 'Here he is!' Do not go running after them. For the Son of Man in his day will be like the lightning which flashes and lights up the sky from one end to the other. But first he must suffer many things and be rejected by this generation. Just as it was in the days of Noah, so also will it be in the days of Noah, so also will it be in the days of the Son of Man. People were eating, drinking, marrying, and being given in marriage up to the day Noah entered the ark. Then the flood came and destroyed them all. It was the same in the days of Lot. People were eating and drinking, buying and selling, planting and building. But the day Lot left Sodom, fire and sulfur rained down from heaven and destroyed them all. It will be just like this on the day of the Son of Man is revealed. On that day, the one who will be on the roof, with his goods in the house, must not go down to take them out; and likewise the one in the field must not turn back. Remember Lot's wife! Whoever tries to keep his life will lose it, whoever loses his life will preserve it. I tell you, on that night two people will be in one bed, one will be taken and the other left. There will be two women grinding at the same place; one will be taken and the other will be left. Two men will be in the field; one will be taken and the other will be left. Where there is a dead body, there the vultures will gather.

PARABLES ON PRAYER
Luke 18
In a certain city there was a judge who did not fear God and did not respect any person. Now there was a widow in that city, and she kept coming to him, saying, 'Give me justice against my opponent.' For a while he was unwilling; but later he said to himself, 'Even though I do not fear God nor respect any person, yet because this widow is bothering me, I will give her justice; otherwise by continually coming she will wear me out. Listen to what the unrighteous judge said; now, will God not bring about justice for His elect who cry out to Him day and night and will He delay long for them? I tell you that He will bring about justice for them quickly. However, when the Son of Man comes, will He find faith on the earth? Two men went up to the temple to pray, one a Pharisee and the other a tax collector. The Pharisee stood up and prayed about himself: 'God, I thank you that I am not like other men— robbers, evildoers, adulterers— or even like this tax collector. I fast twice a week and give a tenth of all I get.' But the tax collector stood at a distance. He would not even look up to heaven, but beat his breast and said, 'God, have mercy on me, a sinner.' I tell you that this man, rather than the other, went home justified before God. For everyone who exalts himself will be humbled, and he who humbles himself will be exalted.

THE PARABLE OF THE VINEYARD WORKERS
Matthew 20

For the kingdom of heaven is like a land over who went out early in the morning to hire men to work in his vineyard. He agreed to pay them a denarius for the day and sent them into his vineyard. About the third hour he went out and saw others standing in the marketplace doing nothing. He told them, 'You also go and work in my vineyard, and I will pay you whatever is right.' So they went. He went out again about the sixth hour and the ninth hour and did the same thing. About the eleventh hour he went out and found still others standing around. He asked them, 'Why have you been standing here all day long doing nothing?'

'Because no one has hired us,' they answered. He said to them, 'You also go and work in my vineyard.' When evening came, the owner of the vineyard said to his foreman, 'Call the workers and pay them their wages, beginning with the last ones hired and going on to the first.' The workers who were hired about the eleventh hour came and each received a denarius. So when those came who were hired first, they expected to receive more. But each one of them also received it, they began to grumble against the landowner. 'These men who were hired last worked only one hour,' they said, 'and you have made them equal to us who have borne the burden of the work and the heat of the day.' But he answered one of them, 'Friend, I am not being unfair to you. Didn't you agree to work for a denarius? Take your pay and go. I want to give the man who was hired last the same as I gave you. Don't I have the right to do what I want with my own money? Or are you envious because I am generous?' So the last will be first, and the first will be last.

ZACCHEUS & THE PARABLE OF THE TEN MINAS
Luke 19

Zaccheus, come down immediately. I must stay at your house today.
Today salvation has come to this house, because this man, too, is a son of Abraham. For the Son of Man came to seek and to save what was lost.
A man of noble birth went to a distant country to have himself appointed king and then to return. So he called ten of his servants and gave them ten minas. 'Put this money to work,' he said, 'until I come back.' But his subjects hated him and sent a delegation after him to say, 'We don't want this man to be our king.' He was made king, however, and returned home. Then he sent for the servants to whom he had given the money, in order to find out what they had gained with it. The first one came and said, 'Sir, your mina has earned ten more.'
'Well done, my good servant!' his master replied. 'Because you have been trustworthy in a very small matter, take charge of ten cities.'

The second came and said, 'Sir, your mina has earned five more.' His master answered, 'You take charge of five cities.'

Then another servant came and said, 'Sir, here is your mina; I have kept it laid away in a piece of cloth. I was afraid of you, because you are a hard man. You take out what you did not put in and reap what you did not sow.' His master replied, 'I will judge you by your own words, you wicked servant! You knew, did you, that I am a hard man, taking out what I did not put in, and reaping what I did not sow? Why then didn't you put my money on deposit, so that when I came back, I could have collected it with interest?'

Then he said to those standing by, 'Take his mina away from him and give it to the one who has 10 minas.'

'Sir,' they said, 'He already has 10!'

He replied, 'I tell you that to everyone who has, more will be given, but as for the one who has nothing, even what he has will be taken away. But those enemies of mine who did not want me to be king over them– bring them here and kill them in front of me.'

JESUS, THE RESURRECTION & THE LIFE
JOHN 11

This sickness will not end in death. No it is for God's glory so that God's son may be glorified through it. Let us go back to Judea. Are there not twelve hours of daylight? A man who walks by day will not stumble, for he sees by this world's light. It is when he walks by night that he stumbles, for he has no light. Our friend Lazarus has fallen asleep; but I am going there to wake him up. Lazarus is dead, and for your sake I am glad I was not there, so that you may believe. But let us go to him.

[To Martha] Your brother will rise from the dead. I am the resurrection and the life. He who believes in me will never die. Do you believe this? Where have you laid him? Take away the stone.

Did I not tell you that if you believed, you would see the glory of God?

Father, I thank you that you have heard me. I knew that you always hear me, but I said this for the benefit of the people standing here, that they may believe that you sent me.

Lazarus! Come out! Take off the grave clothes and let him go.

JESUS ANNOINTED AT BETHANY
John 12
Leave her alone, it was intended that she should save this perfume for the day of my burial. You will always have the poor among you , but you will not always have me.

DEATH & RESURRECTION FORETOLD
Matthew 20 - Mark 11
We are going up to Jerusalem and the Son of Man will be betrayed to the chief priests and teachers of the Law. They will condemn Him to death and will hand Him over to the Gentiles, who will mock Him and spit on Him. Three days later he will be raised to life!

JAMES AND JOHN'S MOTHER'S REQUEST
Matthew 20 - Mark 11
What do you want me to do for you?
You don't know what you are asking. Can you drink the cup I drink or be baptized with the baptism I am baptized with? You will indeed drink from my cup I drink and be baptized with the baptism I am baptized with, but to sit at my right or left is not for me to grant. These places belong to those for whom they have been prepared by my Father. You know the rulers of the Gentiles lord it over them, and their high officials exercise authority over them. Not so with you. Instead, whoever wants to be great among you must be your servant, and whoever wants to be first must be your slave and a slave to all– just as the Son of Man did not come to be served, but to serve, and to give his life as a ransom for many.

THE TRIUMPHAL ENTRY
Matthew 21 - Mark 11 - Luke 19 - John 12
Go to the village ahead of you, and at once you will find a donkey tied there, with her colt by her. Untie them and bring them to me. If anyone says anything to you, tell him that the Lord needs them, and he will send them right away back here shortly.
I tell you, if they keep quiet, the stones will cry out.
If you, even you, had only known on this day what would bring you peace – but now it is hidden from your eyes. The days will come upon you when your enemies will build an embankment against you and encircle you and hem you in on every side. They will dash you to the ground, you and the children within your walls. They will not leave one stone on another, because you did not recognize the time of God's coming to you.

JESUS CURSES THE FIG TREE & CLEANSING THE TEMPLE
Matthew 21 - Mark 11 - Luke 19 - John 2
May no one eat fruit from you and never bear fruit again!
Get out of here! How dare you turn my Father's house into a market! It is written: 'My house will be called a house of prayer for all nations,' but you have made it a den of robbers. Destroy this temple, and I will raise it again in three days. Yes, have you never read, 'From the lips of children and infants you have ordained praise?'
Have faith in God. I tell you the truth, if you have faith and do not doubt, not only can you do what was done to this fig tree, but also anyone can say to this mountain, 'Go, throw yourself into the sea,' and does not doubt in his heart, but believes that what he will say will happen, it will be done for him. Therefore I tell you, whatever you ask for in prayer, believe that you have received it, and it will be yours. And when you stand praying, if you hold anything against anyone, forgive him, so that your heavenly Father may forgive your sins.
I will also ask you one question. Answer me, and I will tell you by what authority I am doing these things. Tell me, John's baptism – where did it come from? Was it from heaven or from men? Neither will I tell you by what authority I am doing these things.

PARABLE OF TWO SONS, LANDOWNER & THE WEDDING FEAST
Matthew 21-22 - Mark 12 - Luke 20
What do you think? There was a man who had two sons. He went to the first and said, 'Son, go and work today in the vineyard.'
'I will not,' he answered, but later he changed his mind and went. Then the father went to the other son and said the same things. He answered, 'I will, sir,' but he did not go. Which of the two did what the Father wanted? I tell you the truth, the tax collectors and prostitutes are entering the kingdom of God ahead of you. For John came to you to show you the way of righteousness and you did not believe him, but the tax collectors and prostitutes did. And even after you saw this, you did not repent and believe him.
Listen to another parable: there was a landowner who planted a vineyard. He built a wall around it, dug a winepress in it and built a watchtower. Then he rented the vineyard to some farmers and went away on a journey. When the harvest time approached, he sent his servants to the tenants to collect his fruit. But the tenants seized him, beat him and sent him away empty-handed. Then he sent another servant to them; they struck him on the head and treated him shamefully. He still sent another, and that one they stoned & killed. He sent many others; some of them they beat, others they killed. He had one left to send, a son, whom he loved.

He sent him last of all, saying 'They will respect my son.' But the tenants said to one another, 'This is their heir. Come, let's kill him, and the inheritance will be ours.' So they took him and killed him, and threw him out of the vineyard. What then will the owner of the vineyard do? He will come and kill those tenants and give the vineyard to others. Haven't you read the Scriptures, 'The stone the builders rejected has become the capstone; the Lord has done this and it is marvelous in our eyes.' Therefore I tell you that the kingdom of God will be taken away from you and given to a people who will produce its fruit. He who falls on this stone will be broken to pieces, but he whom it falls will be crushed.

The kingdom of heaven is like a king who held a wedding feast for his son. And he sent his slaves to call those who had been invited to the wedding feast, and they were unwilling to come. Again he sent other slaves, saying, 'Tell those who have been invited: Behold, I have prepared my dinner; my oxen and my fattened cattle are all butchered and everything is ready. Come to the wedding feast!' But they paid no attention and went their separate ways, one to his own farm, another to his business, and the rest seized his slaves and treated them abusively, and then killed them. Now the king was angry, and he sent his armies and destroyed those murderers, and set their city on fire. Then he said to his slaves, 'The wedding feast is ready, but those who were invited were not worthy. So go to the main roads, and invite whomever you find there to the wedding feast.' Those slaves went out into the streets and gathered together all whom they found, both bad and good; and the wedding hall was filled with dinner guests. But when the king came in to look over the dinner guests, he saw a man who was there who was not dressed in wedding clothes, and he said to him, 'Friend, how did you get in here without wedding clothes?' And the man was speechless. Then the king said to the servants, 'Tie his hands and feet, and throw him into the outer darkness; there will be weeping and gnashing of teeth in that place.' For many are called, but few are chosen.

TAXES TO CAESAR, MARRIAGE & RESURRECTION, THE GREATEST COMMANDMENT, AND THE SON OF DAVID
Matthew 22 - Mark 12 - Luke 20

You hypocrites! Why are you trying to trap me? Show me the coin used for paying the tax. Whose portrait is this? And whose inscriptions? Give to Caesar what is Caesar's, and to God what is God's.

You are in error because you do not know the Scriptures or the power of God, The people of this age marry and are given in marriage, and they can no longer die; for they are like angels. They are God's children, since they are children of the resurrection. But in the account of the bush, even Moses showed that the dead rise, for he calls the Lord:

'The God of Abraham, and the God of Isaac, and the God of Jacob.' He is not the God of the dead, but of the living, for to Him all are alive.

The most important commandment is this: 'Hear, O Israel, the Lord our God, the Lord is one. Love the Lord your God with all your heart and with all your soul and with all your mind and with all your strength.' This is the first and greatest commandment. And the second is like it: 'Love your neighbor as yourself.' All the Law and the Prophets hang on these two commandments. You are not far from the kingdom.

What do you think about the Christ? Whose son is He? How is it then that David, speaking by the Spirit, calls Him 'Lord'? For he says, The Lord said to my lord, sit at my right hand until I put your enemies under your feet.' If then David calls Him 'Lord,' how can he be his son?

THE POOR WIDOW
Mark 12 - Luke 21

I tell you the truth, this poor widow has put more into the treasury than all the others. They all gave gifts out of their wealth; but she, out of her poverty, put in everything– all she had to live on.

WOES & CURSES
Matthew 23

The teacher of the Law and the Pharisees sit in Moses' seat. So you must obey them and do everything they tell you. But do not do what they do, for they do not practice what they preach. They tie up heavy loads and put them on men's shoulders, but they themselves are not willing to lift a finger to move them. Everything they do is done for men to see: They make their phylacteries wide and tassels on their garments long; they love the place of honor at banquets and the most important seats in the synagogues; they love to be greeted in the marketplaces and to have men call them 'rabbi.' But you are not to be called 'rabbi,' for you have only one Master and you are all brothers. And do not call anyone on earth 'father,' for you have only one Father, and he is in heaven. Nor are you to be called 'teacher,' for you have one Teacher, the Christ. The greatest among you will be your servant. For whoever exalts himself will be your servant. For whoever exalts himself will be humbled, and whoever humbles himself will be exalted. Woe to you, teachers of the Law and Pharisees, you hypocrites! You shut the kingdom in men's faces. You yourselves do not enter, nor will you let those enter who are trying to. Woe to you, teachers of the Law and Pharisees, you hypocrites! You devour widow's houses and for a show make lengthy prayers. Therefore you will be punished more severely.

Woe to you, teachers of the Law and Pharisees, you hypocrites! You travel over land and sea to win a single convert, and when he becomes one, you make him twice as much a son of hell as you are.

Woe to you, blind guides! You say, 'if anyone swears by the temple, it means nothing; but if anyone swears by the gold of the temple, he is bound by his oath.' You blind fools! Which is greater: the gold, or the temple that makes the gold sacred? You also say, 'if anyone swears by the altar, it means nothing; but if anyone swears by the gift on it, he is bound by his oath.' You blind men! Which is greater; the gift or the altar that makes the gift sacred? Therefore, he who swears by the altar swear by it and everything on it. And he who swears by the temple swears by it and by the one who dwells in it. And he who swears by heaven, swears by God's throne and by the one who sits on it.

Woe to you, teachers of the Law and Pharisees, you hypocrites! You give a tenth of your spices— mint, dill, and cumin. But you have neglected the more important matters of the Law— justice, mercy, and faithfulness. You should have practiced the latter, without neglecting the former. You blind guides! You strain out a gnat but swallow a camel.

Woe to you, teachers of the Law and Pharisees, you hypocrites! You clean the outside of the cup and dish, but inside they are full of greed and self-indulgence. Blind Pharisee! First clean the inside of the cup and dish, and then the outside will also be clean.

Woe to you, teachers of the Law and Pharisees, you hypocrites! You are like whitewashed tombs, which look beautiful on the outside, but on the inside are full of dead men's bones and everything unclean. In the same way, on the outside you appear as righteous, but on the inside you are full of hypocrisy and wickedness.

Woe to you, teachers of the Law and Pharisees, you hypocrites! You build tombs for the Prophets and decorate the graves of the righteous. And you say, 'If we had lived in the days of our forefathers, we would not have taken part with them shedding the blood of the prophets.' So you testify against yourselves that you are descendents of those who murdered the prophets. Fill up, then, the measure of the sin of your forefathers.

You snakes! You brood of vipers! How will you escape being condemned to hell? Therefore, I am sending you prophets and wise men and teachers. Some of them you will kill and crucify; others you will flog in your synagogues and pursue from town to town. And so upon you will come all the righteous blood that has been shed on earth, from the blood of the righteous Abel to the blood of Zechariah, son of Berekiah, whom you murdered between the temple and the altar. I tell you the truth, all this will come upon this generation.

O Jerusalem, Jerusalem, you will kill the prophets and stone those sent to you, how often I have longed to gather your children together, as a hen gathers her chicks under her wings, but you were not willing. Look, your house is left to you desolate. For I tell you, you will not see men again until you say, 'Blessed is He who comes in the name of the Lord.'

SIGNS AT THE END OF THE AGE
Matthew 24 - Mark 13 - Luke 21

Do you see these great buildings? As for what you see here, I tell you the truth, not one stone will be left on another; every one will be thrown down.

Watch out that no one deceives you. For many will come in My name, claiming, 'I am he,' 'I am the Christ,' and 'The time is near,' and will deceive many. Do not follow them. You will hear of wars, revolutions, and rumors of wars, but see to it that you are not alarmed. Such things must happen first, but the end is still to come. Nation will rise against nation, and kingdom against kingdom. There will be great earthquakes, famines, and pestilences in various places, and fearful events and great signs of heaven. All these are the beginning of the birth pains. But before this, then you will be handed over to be persecuted and put to death and you will be hated by all nations because of me. At that time many will turn away from the faith and will betray and hate each other, and many false prophets will appear and deceive many people. Because of the increase of wickedness, the love of most will grow cold, but he who stands firm to the end will be saved. They will deliver you to the synagogues and prisons, and you will be brought before kings and governors, and all on account of my name. This will result in your being witnesses to them. But make up your mind not to worry before how you will defend yourselves. For the Holy Spirit will give you words and wisdoms, that none of your adversaries will be able to resist or contradict. You will be betrayed even by parents, brothers, relatives, and friends, and they will put some of you to death. All men will hate you because of me. But not a hair on your head will perish. By standing firm you will gain life. So when you see standing in the holy places 'the abomination of desolation,' spoken of through the prophet Daniel– let the reader understand– then let those who are in Judea flee to the mountains. Let no one on the roof of his house go down to take anything out of his house. Let no one in the field go back to get his cloak. How dreadful it will be in those days for pregnant women and nursing mothers! Pray that your flight will not take place in winter or on the Sabbath. For then there will be a great distress, unequaled from the beginning of the world until now– and never to be equaled again. If those days had not been cut short, no one would survive, but for the sake of the elect those days will be shortened.

At that, time if anyone says to you, 'Look, here is the Christ!' or 'There he is!' do not believe it. For false christs and false prophets will appear and perform great signs and miracles or deceive even the elect– if that were possible. See, I have told you ahead of time. So if anyone tells you, 'There he is, out in the desert,' do not go out; or 'Here he is in the inner rooms,' do not believe it. For as lightning that comes from the east is visible even in the west, so will be the coming of the Son of Man. Wherever there is a carcass, there the vultures will gather. They will fall by the sword and will be taken as prisoners to all the nations. Jerusalem will be trampled on by the Gentiles until the times of the Gentiles are fulfilled. Immediately after the distress of those days, 'The sun will be darkened, and the moon will not give its light; the stars will fall from the sky, and the heavenly bodies will be shaken.' At that time the sign of the Son of Man will appear in the sky, and all the nations of the earth will mourn. They will see the Son of Man coming on the clouds of the sky, with power and great glory. And he will send his angels with a loud trumpet call, and they will gather his elect from the four winds, from one end of the heavens to the other: When these things begin to take place, stand up and lift up your heads, because your redemption is drawing near. Now learn this lesson and look at the fig tree and all the trees. When the twigs get tender and sprout leaves, you can see yourselves that summer is near. Even so, when you see these things happening, you know the Kingdom of God is near. I tell you the truth, this generation will certainly not pass away until all these things have happened. Heaven and earth will pass away, but my words will never pass away.

Be careful, or your hearts will be weighed down with dissipation, drunkenness, and the anxieties of life, and that day will close on you unexpectedly like a trap. For it will come upon all those who live on the face of the whole earth. Be always on the watch and pray that you may be able to escape all that is about to happen, and that you may be able to stand before the Son of Man.

No one knows about that day or hour, not even the angels in heaven, nor the Son, but only the Father. As it was in the days of Noah, so it will be at the coming of the Son of Man. For in the days before the flood, people were eating and drinking, marrying and given in marriage, up to the day Noah entered the Ark; and they knew nothing about what would happen until the flood came and took them all away. That is how it will be at the coming of the Son of Man. Two men will be in the field; one will be taken and the other left. Two women will be grinding with a hand mill; one will be taken and the other left. Therefore keep watch, because you do not know on what day your Lord will come. But understand this; if the owner of the house knew at what time of the night the thief was coming, he would have kept watch and would not have let his house be broken into. So you also must be ready, because the Son of Man will come at an hour when you do not expect Him.

Who then is a faithful and wise servant, whom the master has put in charge of the servants in his household to give them their food at the proper time? It will be good for that servant whose master finds him doing so when he returns. I tell you the truth, he will put him in charge of all his possessions. But suppose that servant is wicked and says to himself, 'My master is staying away a long time,' and he then begins to beat his fellow servants and to eat and drink with drunkards. The master of that servant will come on a day when he does not expect him and at an hour he is not aware of. He will cut him to pieces and assign him a place with the hypocrites, where there will be weeping and gnashing of teeth.

Therefore keep watch because you do not know when the owner of the house will come back. Whether in the morning, in the evening, at midnight or when the rooster crows, or at dawn. If he comes suddenly, do not let him find you sleeping. What I say to say, I say to everyone, 'Watch!'

PARABLE OF THE TEN VIRGINS, TALENTS, AND THE SHEEP & GOATS
Matthew 25

At the time of the kingdom of heaven will be like ten virgins who took their lamps and went out to meet the bridegroom. Five of them were foolish and five were wise. The foolish ones toom their lamps, but did not take any oil with them. The wise, however, took oil in jars along with their lamps. The bridegroom was a long time in coming, and they all became drowsy and fell asleep. At the midnight the cry rang out. 'Behold, the bridegroom! Come out to meet him!' Then all the virgins woke up and trimmed their lamps. The foolish ones said to the wise, 'Give us some of your oil; our lamps are going out.'

'No,' they replied, 'there may not be enough for both us and you. Instead, go to those who sell oil and buy some for yourselves.' But while they were on the way to buy the oil, the bridegroom arrived. The virgins who were ready went in with him to the wedding banquet. And the doors were shut. Later the other came, 'Sir! Sir!' They said, 'Open the door for us!'

But he replied, 'I tell you the truth, I don't know you.' Therefore keep watch, because you do not know the day or the hour.

Again, it will be like a man going on a journey, who called his servants and entrusted his property to them. To the one he gave five talents of money, to another two talents, and to another one talent, each according to his ability. Then he went on his journey. The man who had received the five talents went at once and put his money to work and gained five more. So also, the one with the two talents gained two more. But the man who had received the one talent went off, dug a hole in the ground and hid his master's money.

After a long time the master of those servants returned and settled accounts with them. The man who had received the five talents brought the other five. 'Master,' he said, 'you entrusted me with five talents. See, I have gained five more.'

His master replied, 'Well done, good and faithful servant! You have been faithful with a few things; I will put you in charge of many things. Come and share your master's happiness.'

The man with the two talents also came, 'Mater,' he said, 'You entrusted me with two talents; See, I have gained two more.'

His master replied, 'Well done, good and faithful servant! You have been faithful with a few things; I will put you in charge of many things. Come and share your master's happiness!'

Then the man who had received the one talent came. 'Master,' he said, 'I know you are a hard man, harvesting where you have not sown and gathering where you have not scattered seed. So I was afraid and went out and hid your talent in the ground. See, here is what belongs to you.'

His master replied, 'You wicked, lazy servant! So you knew I harvest where I have not sown and gather where I have not scattered seed? Well then, you should have put my money on deposit with the bankers, so that when I returned I would have received it back with interest. Take that talent from him and give it to the one who has ten talents. For everyone, who has will be given more, and he will have an abundance. Whoever does not have, even what he has will be taken from him. And throw that worthless servant outside; into the outer darkness, where there will be weeping and gnashing of teeth.'

When the Son of Man comes in His glory and all the angels with Him, He will sit on the throne in heavenly glory. All the nations will be gathered before Him, and He will separate one from another as a shepherd separates the sheep from the goats. He will put the sheep on his right and the goats on his left. Then the King will say to those on his right, 'Come, you who are blessed by my Father; take your inheritance, the kingdom prepared for you since the creation of the world. For I was hungry and you gave me something to eat, I was thirsty and you gave me something to drink, I was a stranger and you invited me in, I was naked and you clothed me, I was sick and you looked after me. I was in prison and you came to visit me!'

Then the righteous will answer Him, 'Lord when did we see you hungry and feed you, or thirsty and give you something to drink? When did we see you a stranger and invite you in, or naked and clothe you? When did we see you sick or in prison and go to visit you?

The king will reply, 'I tell you the truth, whatever you did for one of the least of these brothers of mine, you did it for me.'

Then those on his left, 'Depart from me, you who are cursed, into the eternal fire prepared for the devil and his angels for I was hungry, and you gave me nothing to eat, I was thirsty and you gave me nothing to drink, I was a stranger and you did not invite me in, I was naked and you did not clothe me, I was sick and in prison and you did not look after me.'
They will answer, 'Lord, when did we see you hungry or thirsty or a stranger or needing clothes or sick or in prison, and did not help you?
He will reply, 'I tell you the truth, whatever you did not do for one of the least of these, you did not do for me.' Then they will go away to eternal punishment, but the righteous to eternal life.

WOMAN ANOINTS JESUS FOR BURIAL
Matthew 26 - Mark 14
As you know, the Passover is two days away– and the Son of Man will be handed over to be crucified.
Leave her alone, why are you bothering her? She has done a beautiful thing to me. The poor you will always have with you, and you can help them any time you want. But you will not always have me. She did what she could. She poured perfume on my body beforehand to prepare for my burial. I tell you the truth, wherever the gospel is preached throughout the world, what she has done will also be told, in memory of her.

GREEKS SEEK JESUS & JESUS FORETELLS HIS DEATH
John 12
The hour has come for the Son of Man to be glorified. I tell you the truth, unless a kernel of wheat falls to the ground and dies, it remains only a single seed. But if it dies, it produces many seeds. The man who loves his life will lose it, while the man who hates his life in this world will keep it for eternal life. Whoever serves me must follow me; and where I am, my servant also will be. My Father will honor the one who serves me. Now my heart is troubled, and what shall I say? 'Father, save me from this hour'? No, it was for this very reason I came to this hour. Father, glorify your name!
I HAVE GLORIFIED IT, AND WILL GLORIFY IT AGAIN.
This voice was for your benefit, not mine. Now is the time for judgement on this world; now the prince of this world will be driven out. But I, when I am lifted up from the earth, will draw all men to myself. You're going to have the light a little longer. Walk while you have the light, before darkness overtakes you. The man who walks in the dark does not know where he is going. Put your trust in the light while you have it, so that you may become sons of light.

When a man believes in me, he does not believe in me only, but in the one who sent me. When he looks at me, he sees the one who sent me. I have come into the world as a light, so that no one who believes in me should stay in darkness. As for the person who hears my words but does not keep them, I do not judge him. For I did not come to judge the world, but to save it. There is a judge for the one who rejects me and does not accept my words; that very word which I spoke will condemn him at the last day. For I did not speak of my own accord, but the Father who sent me commanded me what I say and how to say it. I know that his command leads to eternal life. So whatever I say is just what the Father has told me to say.

PASSOVER: PREPARATIONS
Matthew 26 - Mark 14 - Luke 22

Go and make preparations for us to eat the Passover. As you enter the city, a man carrying a jar of water will meet you. Follow him to the house that he enters, and say to the owner of the house, 'The Teacher says: My appointed time is near. I am going to celebrate the Passover with my disciples.' He will show you a large upper room, all furnished. Make preparations there.

PASSOVER: JESUS WASHES HIS DISCIPLES' FEET
John 13

You do not realize now what I am doing, but later you will understand. Unless I wash you, you have no part with me. A person who has a bath needs only to wash his feet; his whole body is clean. And you are clean, though not every one of you. Do you understand what I have done for you? You call me 'Teacher' and 'Lord' and rightly so, for that is what I am. Now that I, your Lord and Teacher, have washed your feet, you should also wash one another's feet. I have set you an example that you should do as I have done for you. I tell you the truth, no servant is greater than his master, nor is a messenger greater than the one who sent him. Now that you know these things, you will be blessed if you do them. I am not referring to all of you; I know those I have chosen. But this is to fulfill the Scripture: 'He who shares my bread has lifted up his heel against me.' I am telling you now before it happens, so that when it does happen you will believe that I am He. I tell you the truth, whoever accepts anyone I send accepts me; and whoever accepts me accepts the one who sent me.

PASSOVER: JESUS PREDICTS HIS BETRAYAL
Matthew 26 - Mark 14 - Luke 22 - John 13
I have eagerly desired to eat this Passover with you before I suffer. For I tell you, I will not eat it again until it finds fulfilment in the kingdom of God. Take this and divide it among you. For I tell you, I will not drink again of the fruit of the vine until the kingdom of God comes. This is my body given for you; do this in remembrance of me. This cup is the new covenant in my blood, which is poured out for you. But the hand of him who is going to betray me is with mine on the table. The Son of Man will go as it has been decreed, but woe to that man who betrays him.
I tell you the truth, one of you will betray me– one who is eating with me. It is one of the Twelve, the one who has dipped his hand into the bowl with me will betray me. The Son of Man will go just as it is written about Him. But woe to that man who betrays the Son of Man! It would be better for him if he had not been born. You yourself have said it. What you are about to do, do quickly.

PASSOVER: _____ ONE ANOTHER
Matthew 26 - Mark 14 - Luke 22 - John 13
The king of the Gentiles lord it over them; and those who exercise authority over them call them Benefactors. But you are not to be like that. Instead, the greatest among you should be like the youngest, and the one who rules like the one who serves. For who is greater, the one who is at the table or the one who serves? Is it not the one who is at the table? But I am among you as one who serves. You are those who have stood by me in my trials. And I confer on you a kingdom, just as my Father conferred one on me, so that you may eat and drink at my table in my kingdom and sit on thrones, judging the twelve tribes of Israel. Now is the Son of Man glorified and God is glorified in Him. If God is glorified in Him, God will glorify the Son in Himself, and will glorify Him at once. My children, I will be with you only a little longer. You will look for me, and just as I told the Jews, so I tell you now: Love one another, as I have loved you, so much love one another. By this all men will know that you are my disciples, if you love one another. This very night you all will fall away on account of me, for it is written: 'I will strike the shepherd, and the sheep of the flock will be scattered.' But after I have risen, I will go ahead of you into Galilee. Where I am going, you cannot follow now, but you will follow later.
Simon, Simon, Satan has asked to sift you all as wheat. But I have prayed for you, Simon, that your faith may not fail. And when you have turned back, strengthen your brothers. I tell you, Peter, before the rooster crows today, you will disown and deny me three times that you know me.

When I sent you without a purse, bag or sandals, did you lack anything? But now if you have a purse, take it, and also a bag; and if you don't have a sword, sell your cloak and buy one. It is written: 'And he was numbered with the transgressors; and I tell you that this must be fulfilled in me. Yes, what is written about me is reaching its fulfillment. That is enough.

JESUS, THE WAY, THE TRUTH, THE LIFE
John 14
Do not let your hearts be troubled. Trust in God, trust also in me. In my Father's house are many rooms; if it were not so, I would have told you. I am going there to prepare a place for you. I will come back and take you to be with Me that you also may be where I am. You know the way to the place where I am going.
I am the way and the truth and the life. No one comes to the Father except through Me. If you really know Me, you would know My Father as well. From now on, you do know Him and have seen Him. Do you know me, Philip, even after I have been among you such a long time? Anyone who has seen Me has seen the Father. How can you say, 'show us the Father'? Don't you believe that I am in the Father, and that the Father is in Me? The words I say to you are not just My own. Rather, it is the Father, living in Me, who is doing His work. Believe me when I say that I am in the Father and the Father is in Me; or at least believe in the evidence of the miracles themselves. I tell you the truth, anyone who has faith in Me will do what I have been doing. He will do even greater things than these, because I am going to the Father. And I will do whatever you ask in My name, so that the Son may bring glory to the Father. You may ask Me for anything in My name, and I will do it. If you love Me, you will obey what I command. And I will ask the Father, and He will give you another Counselor to be with you forever– the Spirit of truth. The world cannot accept Him, because it neither sees Him nor knows Him. But you know Him, for He lives with you and will be in you. I will not leave you as orphans; I will come to you. Before long, the world will not see Me anymore, but you will see Me. Because I live, you also will live. On that day you will realize that I am in My Father, and you are in Me, and I am in you. Whoever has My commands and obeys them, he is the one who loves Me. He who loves Me will be loved by My Father, and I too will love him and show Myself to him. If anyone loves Me, he will obey my teaching. My Father will love him, and We will come to him and make Our home with him. He who does not love Me will not obey My teachings. These words you hear are not My own; they belong to the Father who sent Me. All this I have spoken while still with you. But the Counselor, the Holy Spirit, whom the Father will send in My name, will teach you all things and will remind you of everything I have said to you.

Peace I leave with you; My peace I give you. I do not give to you as the world gives. Do not let your hearts be troubled and do not be afraid. You heard Me say, 'I am going away and I am coming back to you.' If you loved Me, you would be glad that I am going to the Father, for the Father is greater than I. I have told you now before it happens, so that when it does happen you will believe. I will not speak with you much longer, for the prince of this world coming. He has no hold on Me, but the world must learn that I love the Father and that I do exactly what My Father has commanded Me. Come now let us leave.

JESUS, THE VINE
John 15

I am the true vine, and My Father is the gardener. He cuts off every branch in Me that does not bear fruit, while every branch that does bear fruit he prunes so that it will be even more fruitful. You are already clean because of the word I have spoken to you. Remain in Me and I will remain in you. No branch can bear fruit unless you remain in Me. I am the vine, you are the branches. If a man remains in Me and I in him, he will bear much fruit; apart from Me you can do nothing. If anyone does not remain in Me, he is like a branch that is thrown away and withers; such branches are picked up, thrown into the fire and burned. If you remain in Me and My words remain in you, ask what you wish, and it will be given you. This is to My Father's glory, that you bear much fruit, showing yourselves to be My disciples. As the Father has loved Me, so I have loved you. Now remain in My love. If you obey My commands, you will remain in My love, just as I have obeyed My Father's commands and remain in His love. I have told you this so that My joy may be in you and that your joy may be complete. My command is this: Love each other as I have loved you. Greater love has no one than this, that he lay down his life for his friends. You are My friends if you do what I command. I no longer call you servants, because a servant does not know his master's business. Instead, I have called you friends, for everything that I learned from My Father, I have made known to you. You did not choose Me, but I chose you and appointed you to go and bear fruit– fruit that will last. Then the Father will give you whatever you ask in My name. This is My command: Love each other. If the world hates you, keep in mind that it hated Me first. If you belonged to the world, it would love you as its own. As it is, you do not belong to the world, but I have chosen you out of the world, that is why the world hates you. Remember the words I spoke to you: 'No servant is greater than his master.' If they persecuted Me, they will persecute you also. They will treat you this way because of My name, for they do not know the One who sent Me. If I had not come and spoken to them, they would not be guilty of sin. Now, however, they have no excuse for their sin.

He who hates Me hates My Father as well. If I had not done among them the works that no one else did, then they would not be guilty of sin. But now they have seen these miracles, and yet they have both hated Me and My Father. But this fulfills what is written in their Law: 'They hated me without reason.'
When the Counselor comes, whom I will send to you from the Father, the Spirit of Truth who goes out from My Father, He will testify about Me. And you also must testify, for you have been with Me from the beginning.

SORROW TURNED TO JOY
John 16
All this I have told you so that you will not go astray. They will put you out of the synagogue, in fact, a time is coming when anyone who kills you will think he is offering a service to God. They will do such things because they have not known the Father or Me. I have told you this, so that when the time comes you will remember that I warned you. I did not tell you this at first because I was with you. Now I am going to Him who sent Me, yet none of you asks Me, 'Where are you going?' Because I have said these things, you are filled with grief. But I tell you the truth; It is for your good that I am going away. Unless I go away, the Counselor will not come to you; but if I go, I will send Him to you. When He comes, He will convict the world in regard to sin and righteousness and judgement. In regard to sin, because men do not believe in me; in regard to righteousness, because I am going to the Father where you can see Me no longer; and in regard to judgement, because the prince of the world now stands condemned. I have much more to say to you, more than you can bear. But when He, the Spirit of Truth, comes, He will guide you into all truth. He will not speak on His own; He will speak only what He hears, and He will tell you what is to come. He will bring glory to Me by taking from what is Mine and making it known to you. All that belongs to the Father is Mine. That is why I said the Spirit will take from what is Mine and make it known to you. In a little while you will see Me no more, and then after a little while you will see Me.
Are you asking one another what I meant when I said, 'In a little while you will see Me no more, and then after a little while you will see Me'? I tell you the truth, you will weep and mourn while the world rejoices. You will grieve, but your grief will turn into joy. A woman giving birth to a child has pain because her time has come; but when her baby is born she forgets the anguish because of her joy that a child is born into the world. So with you: Now is your time of grief, but I will see you again and you will rejoice, and no one will take away your joy. In that day you will no longer ask Me anything. I tell you the truth, My Father will give you whatever you ask in My name. Until now you have not asked for anything in My name.

Ask and you will receive, and your joy will be complete. Though I have been speaking figuratively, a time is coming when I will no longer use this kind of language but will tell you plainly about My Father. In that day you will ask in My name, I am not saying that I will ask the Father on your behalf. No, the Father Himself loves you because you have loved Me and have believed that I came from the Father and entered the world; now I am leaving the world and going back to the Father.

You believe at last! But a time is coming, and has come, when you will be scattered each to his own home. You will leave Me all alone. Yet I am not alone, for My Father is with Me. I have told you these things, so that in Me you may have peace. In this world you will have trouble. But take heart! I have overcome the world.

JESUS PRAYS IN THE GARDEN OF GETHSEMANE
Matthew 26 - Mark 14 - Luke 22 - John 17

Sit here while I go over there and pray. My soul is overwhelmed with sorrow to the point of death. Stay here and keep watch with me. Abba, if You are willing, My Father, if it is possible, may this cup be taken from Me. Yet not as I will, but what You will.

Simon, are you asleep? Could you men not keep watch with me for one hour? Get up, watch and pray so that you will not fall into temptation. The spirit is willing, but the flesh is weak.

Father, the time has come. Glorify Your Son that Your Son may glorify You. For You granted Him authority over all people that He might give eternal life to all those you have given Him. Now this is eternal life: that they may know You, the only true God, and Jesus Christ, whom You have sent. I have brought You glory on earth by completing the work You gave Me to do. And now, Father, glorify Me in Your presence with the glory I had with You before the world began. I have revealed to You, Your name, to those whom You gave Me out of the world. They were Yours: You gave them to Me and they have obeyed Your word. Now they know that everything You have given Me comes from You. For I gave them the words You gave Me and they accepted them. They knew with certainty that I came from You, and they believed that You sent Me. I pray for them. I am not praying for the world, but for those You have given Me, for they are Yours. All I have is Yours, and all You have is Mine. And glory has come to Me through them. I will remain in the world no longer, but they are still in the world, and I am coming to You. Holy Father, protect them by the power of Your name– the name you gave Me– so that they may be one as We are one. While I was with them, I protected them and kept them safe by that name you gave Me. None has been lost except the one doomed to destruction so that Scripture would be fulfilled.

I am coming to You now, but I say these things while I am still in the world, so that they may have the full measure of joy within them. I have given them Your word and the world has hated them, for they are not of the world anymore than I am of the world. My prayer is not that You take them out of the world, but that you protect them from the evil one. They are not of the world, even as I am not of it. Sanctify them by the truth; Your word is truth. As You sent Me into the world, I have sent them into the world. For them I sanctify Myself, that they too may be truly sanctified. My prayer is not for them alone. I pray also for those who will believe in Me through their message, that all of them may be one. Father, just as You are in Me and I am in You. May they also be in Us so that the world may believe that You have sent Me. I have given them the glory that You have gave Me, that they may be one as We are one. I in them and You in Me. May they be brought to complete unity to let the world know that You sent Me and have loved them even as You have loved Me. Father, I want those You have given Me to be with Me where I am, and to see My glory, the glory you have given Me because You loved Me before the creation of the world. Righteous Father, though the world does not know that You have sent Me. I have made You known to them, and will continue to make You known in order that the love You have for Me may be in them and that I Myself may be in them.

JUDAS BETRAYS JESUS
Matthew 26 - Mark 14 - Luke 22 - John 18
Are you still sleeping and resting? Enough! The hour has come. Look, the Son of Man is betrayed into the hands of sinners. Rise! Let us go! Here comes My betrayer!
Judas, are you betraying the Son of Man with a kiss? Who is it you want? Friend, do what you came for.
I am He. Who is it you want? I told you I am He, if you are looking for Me let these men go.
No more of this! Put your swords away. Shall I not drink the cup the Father has given me? Am I leading a rebellion that you have come out with swords and clubs to capture me? Every day I sat in the temple courts teaching, and you did not arrest me. But this has all taken place that the writings of the Prophets might be fulfilled. But this is your hour when darkness reigns.

JESUS BEFORE ANNAS
John 18
I have spoken openly to the world, I always taught in synagogues or at the temple, where all the Jews come together. I said nothing in secret. Why question me?

Ask those who heard me. Surely they know what I said. If I have spoken wrongly, testify of the wrong; but if rightly, why do you strike me?

JESUS BEFORE THE SANHEDRIN
Matthew 26 - Mark 14 - Luke 22
If I tell you, you will not believe me, and if I asked you, you would not answer. But from now on, the Son of Man will be seated on the right hand of the mighty God. You have said it yourself. You say correctly that I am; and you shall see the Son of Man sitting at the right hand of power, and coming with the clouds of heaven.

JESUS BEFORE PILATE
Matthew 27 - Mark 15 - Luke 23 - John 18-19
Is that your own idea? Or did others talk to you about me? My kingdom is not of this world. If it were, my servants would fight to prevent my arrest by the Jews. But as it is, my kingdom is from another place.
Yes it is as you say. You are right in saying I am a king. In fact, for this reason I was born, and for this I came into the world, to testify to the truth. Everyone on the side of truth listens to me.
You have no power over me if it were not given to you from above. Therefore the one who handed me over to you is guilty of a greater sin.

JESUS CARRYING THE CROSS UP TO GOLGOTHA
Luke 23
Daughters of Jerusalem, do not weep for me; weep for yourselves and for your children. For the time will come when you will say, 'Blessed are the barren women, the wombs that never bore and the breasts that never nursed!' Then they will say to the mountains. 'Fall on us!' and to the hills, 'cover us!' for if men do these things when the tree is green, what will happen when it is dry?

THE CRUCIFIXION & DEATH OF JESUS
Matthew 27 - Mark 15 - Luke 23 - John 19
Father, forgive them, for they know not what they are doing.
My God! My God! Why have you forsaken me? (eloi, eloi, lama sabachthani)
Dear woman, here is your son. Here is your mother.
I am thirsty.
I tell you the truth, today you will be with me in paradise.
Father, into your hands I commit My Spirit.
It is finished.

THE RESURRECTION OF JESUS & APPEARING TO HIS DISCIPLES
Matthew 28 - Luke 24 - John 20-21

Woman, why are you crying? Who is it you are looking for? Mary. Do not hold on to Me, for I have not yet returned to the Father. Go instead to My brothers and tell them to go to Galilee; there they will see Me. Say to them also, 'I am returning to My Father and your Father, to My God and your God.

What are you discussing together as you walk along? What things? How foolish you are, and how slow of heart to believe all that the prophets have spoken! Did not the Christ have to suffer these things and then enter His glory?

Peace be with you. Receive the Holy Spirit. If you forgive anyone his sins, they are forgiven; if you do not forgive them, they are not forgiven.

Why are you troubled, and why do doubts rise in your minds? Look at my hands and my feet. It is I myself! Touch me and see; a ghost does not have flesh and bones, as you see I have. Do you still have anything here to eat?

This is what I told you while I was still with you: Everything must be fulfilled that is written about Me in the Law of Moses, the Prophets and the Psalms. This is what is written: The Christ will suffer and rise from the dead on the third day, and repentance and forgiveness of sins will be preached in His name to all nations, beginning at Jerusalem. You are My witnesses of these things. I am going to send you what My Father has promised; but stay in the city until you have been clothed with power from on high! Peace be with you. Put your finger here; see My hands. Reach out your hand and put it into My side. Stop doubting and believe. Because you have seen Me, you have believed; blessed are those who have not seen and yet have believed.

Friend, haven't you any fish? Throw your net on the right side of the boat and you will find some. Bring some of the fish you have just caught. Come and have breakfast.

Simon son of John, do you truly love me more than these? Feed my lambs.

Simon son of John, do you truly love me? Take care of my sheep.

Simon son of John, do you love me? Feed my sheep. I tell you the truth, when you were younger you dressed yourself and went where you wanted; but when you are old you will stretch out your hands, and someone will dress you and lead you where you do not want to go. Follow me.

If I want him to remain alive until I return, what is that to you? You must follow me.

THE GREAT COMMISSION
Matthew 28 - Mark 16

Therefore go into all the world and preach good news to all creation.

Whoever believes and is baptized will be saved, but whoever does not believe will be condemned. Therefore go and make disciples of all nations, baptizing them in the name of the Father and of the Son and of the Holy Spirit and teaching them to obey anything I have commanded you. And surely I am with you always, to the very end of the age. And these signs will accompany those who believe: In My name they will drive out demons; with their hands; and when they drink deadly poison, it will not hurt them at all; they will place their hands on sick people, and they will get well.

WAIT ON THE HOLY SPIRIT
Acts 1

Do not leave Jerusalem, but wait for the gift my Father promised, which you have heard me speak about. For John baptized with water, but in a few days you will be baptized with the Holy Spirit. It is not for you to know the times or dates the Father has set by His own authority. But you will receive power when the Holy Spirit comes on you; and you will be my witnesses in Jerusalem, and in all Judea and Samaria, and to the ends of the earth.

THE SPIRIT TO PHILIP
ACTS 8

Go over and join this chariot.

JESUS CALLS SAUL & ANANIAS
Acts 9

Saul, Saul, why are you persecuting Me? I am Jesus the Nazarene whom you are persecuting, but get up and enter the city of Damascus and it will be told you what you must do.

Ananias. Get up and go to the street called Straught, and inquire at the house of Judas for a man from Tarsus named Saul, for he is praying, and he has seen in a vision a man named Ananias come in and lay his hands on him, so that he might regain his sight. Go for he is a chosen instrument of Mine, to bear My name before the Gentiles and kings and the Sons of Israel; for I will show him how much he must suffer on behalf of My name.

THE SPIRIT CALLS PETER TO MEET CORNELIUS
Acts 10

Behold, three men are looking for you. But get up, go downstairs and accompany them without misgivings, for I have sent them Myself.

THE SPIRIT SENDS OUT PAUL & BARNABAS
Acts 13
Set Barnabas and Saul apart for Me for the work to which I have called them.

AGABUS PROPHESIES OVER PAUL
Acts 21
In this way the Jews in Jerusalem will bind the man who owns this belt and hand him over to the Gentiles.

PAUL'S DEFENSE TO THE JEWS
Acts 22-23
Hurry and get out of Jerusalem quickly, because they will not accept your testimony about Me. Go! For I will send you far away to the Gentiles.
Be courageous! For as you have testified to the truth about me in Jerusalem, so you must testify in Rome also.

THE REVELATION OF JESUS CHRIST: THE MESSAGE TO THE SEVEN CHURCHES
Revelation 1-3
I am the Alpha and the Omega, who is and who was and who is to come, the Almighty.
Do not be afraid; I am the first and the last, and the living One; and I was dead, and behold, I am alive forevermore, and I have the keys of death and of Hades. Therefore write the things which you have seen, and the things which are, and the things which will take place after all things. As for the mystery of the seven stars which you saw in My right hand, and the seven golden lampstands: the seven stars are the angels of the seven churches and the seven lampstands are the seven churches.
To the angel of the church in Ephesus while: The One who holds the seven stars in this right hand, the one who walks among the seven golden lampstands, says this: 'I know your deeds and your labor and perseverance, and that you cannot tolerate evil people, and you have put those who call themselves apostles to the test, but are not, and you found them to be false; and you have perseverance and have endured on account of My name, and have not become weary. But I have this against you, that you have left your first love. Therefore, remember from where you have fallen, and repent, and do the deeds you did at first; or else I am coming to you and I will remove your lampstand from its place unless you repent. But have this, that you hate the deeds of the Nicolaitans, which I also hate. The one who has an ear, let him hear what the Spirit says to the churches.

To the one who overcomes, I will grant to eat from the tree of life, which is in the Paradise of God.

And to the angel of the church in Smyrna write: The first and the last, who was dead, and has come to life, says this: I know your tribulation and your poverty (but you are rich), and the slander by those who say they are Jews and are not, but are a synagogue of Satan. Do not fear what you are about to suffer. Behold, the devil is about to throw some of you into prison, so that you will be tested, and you will have tribulation for ten days. Be faithful until death, and I will give you the crown of life. The one who has an ear, let him hear what the Spirit says to the churches. The one who overcomes will not be hurt by the second death.

And to the angel of the church in Pergamum write: The One who has the sharp two-edged sword says this: I know where you dwell, where Satan's throne is; and you hold firmly to My name, and did not deny My faith even in the days of Antipas, My witness, My faithful one, who was killed among you, where Satan dwells. But I have a few things against you, because you have some there who hold to the teaching of Balaam, who kept teaching Balak to put a stumbling block before the Sons of Israel, to eat things sacrificed to idols and to commit sexual immorality. So you too, have some who in the same way hold to the teachings of the Nicolaitans. Therefore repent; or else I am coming to you quickly, and I will wage war against them with the sword of My mouth. The one who has ears, let him hear what the Spirit says to the churches. To the one who overcomes, I will give some of the hidden manna, and I will give him a white stone, and a new name written on the stone which no one knows except the one who receives it!

And to the angel of the church in Thyatira write: The Son of God, who has eyes like flames of fire, and feet like burnished bronze, say this: I know your deeds, and your love and faith, and service and perseverance, and that your deeds of late are greater than at first. But I have this against you, that you tolerate that woman Jezebel, who calls herself a prophetess, and she teaches and leads My bondservants astray so that they commit sexual immorality and eat things sacrificed to idols. I gave her time to repent, and she does not want to repent of her sexual immorality. Behold, I will throw her on a bed of sickness, and those who commit adultery with her into great tribulation, unless they repent of her deeds. And I will kill her children with plague, and all the churches will know that I am He who searches the minds and hearts; and I will give to each one of you according to your deeds. But I say to you, the rest who are in Thyatira, who do not hold to this teaching; who have not known the deep things of Satan, as they call them— I place no other burden on you. Nevertheless what you have, hold firmly until the end, I will give him authority over the nations; and he shall rule them with a rod of iron, as the vessels of the potter are shattered, as I also have received authority from My

Father; and I will give him the morning star. The one who has an ear, let him hear what the Spirit says to the churches.

To the angel of the church in Sardis write: He who has the seven spirits of God and the seven stars, say this: I know your deeds, that you have a name that you are alive, and yet you are dead. Be constantly alert, and strengthen the things that remain, which were about to die; for I have not found your deeds completed in the sight of My God. So remember what you have received and heard; and keep it, and repent. Then if you are not alert, I will come like a thief, and you will not know at what hour I will come to you. But you have a few people in Sardis who have not soiled their garments; and they will walk with Me in white, for they are worthy. Then one who overcomes will be clothed the same way, in white garments; and I will not erase his name from the book of life, and I will confess his name before My Father and before His angels. The one who has an ear, let him hear what the Spirit says to the churches.

And to the angel of the church in Philadelphia write: He who is holy, who is true, who has the key of David, who opens and no one will shut, and who shuts and no one opens, say this: I know your deed. Behold, I have put before you an open door which no one can shut, because you have little power, and have followed My word, and have not denied My name. Behold, I will make those of the synagogue of Satan, who say that they are Jews and are not, but lie– I will make them come and bow before your feet, and make them know that I have loved you. Because you have kept My word of perseverance, I also will keep you from the hour of the testing, that hour which is about to come upon the whole world, to test those who live on the earth. I am coming quickly; hold firmly to what you have, so that no one will take your crown. The one who overcomes, I will make him a pillar in the temple of My God, and he will not go out from it anymore; and I will write on him the name of My God, and the name of the city of My God, the new Jerusalem, which comes down out of heaven from My God, and My new name. The one who has an ear, let him hear what the Spirit says to the churches.

To the angel of the church in Laodicea write: The Amen, the faithful and true Witness, the Origin of the creation of God, says this: I know your deeds, that you are neither cold nor hot; I wish that you were cold or hot. So because you are lukewarm, and neither hot nor cold, I will vomit you out of My mouth. Because you say, 'I am rich, and have become wealthy, and have no need of anything.' and you do not know that you are wretched, miserable, poor, blind, and naked, I advise you to buy from Me gold refined by fire so that you may become rich, and white garments so that you may clothe yourself and the shame of your nakedness will not revealed; and eye salve to apply to your eyes so that you may see. Those whom I

love, I rebuke and discipline; therefore be zealous and repent. Behold, I stand at the door and knock; if anyone hears my voice and opens the door, I will come in to him and will dine with him, and he with Me. The one who overcomes, I will grant to him to sit with Me on My throne, as I also overcame and sat with My Father on His throne. The one who has an ear let him hear what the Spirit says to the churches.

THE SPIRIT TO THE MARTYRS
Revelation 14
Write: Blessed are the dead who die in the Lord from now on! Yes, so that they may rest from their labors, for their deeds follow with them.

THE LAST OF THE BOWLS OF WRATH
Revelation 16
It is done!

THE NEW HEAVENS & THE NEW EARTH
Revelation 21
Behold, I am making all things new. Write, for these words are faithful and true. It is done. I am the Alpha and the Omega, the beginning and the end. I will give water to the one who thirsts from the spring of the water of life, without cost. The one who overcomes will inherit these things, and I will be his God and he will be My son. But for the cowardly, and unbelieving, and abominable, and murderers, and sexually immoral persons, and sorcerers, and idolaters, and all liars, their part will be in the lake that burns with fire and brimstone, which is the second death.

EDEN RESTORED
Revelations 22
And behold, I am coming quickly. Blessed is the one who keeps the words of the prophecy of this book.
Behold, I am coming quickly, and My reward is with Me, to reward each one as his work deserves. I am the Alpha and the Omega, the first and the last, the beginning and the end. I, Jesus, have sent My angel to testify to you of these things for the churches. I am the root and the descendant of David, the bright morning star.
Come.
Yes, I am coming quickly.

Made in the USA
Columbia, SC
01 July 2025